D1344162

THE
KIDGATE STORY

by

David N Robinson OBE MSc

Published by

⬛outh ⬛aturalists', ⬛ntiquarian and ⬛iterary ⬛ociety

The Museum, 4 Broadbank, Louth, Lincs LN11 6EQ
(Tel: 01507 601211)
1997

© David N Robinson 1997

ISBN 0 9520117 5 1

Dedication

To the staff and pupils
who have contributed to the success
of Kidgate School over the last 156 years

Cover photograph by Harold Jackson (1989)

Back cover: The British School
from William Brown's Panorama of Louth (1844)

All rights reserved. No part of this book may be reproduced, stored in a retrieval system, nor transmitted in any form nor by any means, electronic, mechanical, photocopying, whether recording or otherwise, without the prior permission in writing of the copyright holder or his authorised agent.

Text set in Baskerville Book by Penny Dixon

Printed in Great Britain by Allinson & Wilcox
Queen Street, Louth, Lincolnshire LN11 9BN Tel: 01507 606661

Contents

Foreword

To be Headteacher at the town's second oldest school is a great privilege and very rewarding. You only have to walk through its classrooms and corridors to gain a sense of history. You can almost feel the many pupils and staff who have been associated with Kidgate following you. Its 156 years of history is all around you. Of course Kidgate has moved forward over the years educationally and has gained new buildings, but the sense of tradition and values have remained as a tangible reminder of those who founded our school. They did not have an easy time establishing the British School, as it was known in 1841, with opposition from many stating that the poor should not be educated lest they rose above their station. But rise they did and as the school is still growing its future is well assured. Its history, traditions and values all come through in David Robinson's history of the British School.

For those who attended Kidgate it is a must and for those who love Louth it is part of our heritage, and as such essential reading, but above all it is a fascinating insight into a Louth School. To David, Ken and Harold from Kidgate School past and present our grateful thanks.

July 1997   Stuart Sizer, Headteacher

Introduction and Acknowledgements

KIDGATE SCHOOL has a longer history than any other school in the town except the King Edward VI School. The early private schools have disappeared, as have the National Schools in Westgate and Broadbank and the Wesleyan Day School on Newmarket, and Eastfield Road (1865) and St. Michael's (1876) came later than Kidgate which celebrated 150 years in 1991. Not only that, but it established a reputation for sound teaching and for achieving better scholarship results than other junior schools in the town.

This story of the school is very much about people - teachers and pupils. It describes the changing life of the school, both inside the classroom and outside, the payment-by-results years and the scholarship years, the ailments and even the effects of vagaries of the weather. The controversy preceding foundation of the school is taken from Rex Russell's "History of Schools and Education in Lindsey 1800-1902: The foundation and maintenance of schools for the poor" (1965), and other supporting detail from directories and newspapers. The main sources of information were an early managers' minute book (1857 to 1883) and six logbooks for the boys, girls, infants and when it became a mixed school, covering a century from the 1860s to the 1960s. Changes over the last thirty years have been less dramatic and have been left to a future historian to study.

I am much indebted to Harold Jackson and Ken Sidebotham for transcribing the minute book and logbooks which had been deposited in the Lincolnshire Archives; without them this book would not have been possible. Harold also traced the occupations of a number of former pupils from the 1930s and 1940s: they went into business locally (32), haulage (9), building (13), farming (7), teaching (8), nursing (4) and office work (5). This sample analysis clearly shows the impact of Kidgate scholars on the local community. I am also grateful to former pupils who contributed reminiscences of their time at the school, and produced photographs of classes and school activities for copying and inclusion in the book. And to the present headmaster, Stuart Sizer, for writing the Foreword.

FIRST DAY AT SCHOOL

Walking up the hill,
And there it is as still as still,
In through the gates and up to the wall,
The bigger kids are playing football.
Then I feel cold,
And miles from home,
Until I feel a small hand hold,
It is my friend she's all in blue
And both of us feel very new.

EMILY STRATFORD

(from Kidgate News 1991)

In The Beginning

PARADISE it was called. Few children regard school as paradise, but that was the name of the site where the British School was built in 1840-41. Today it is more familiarly known as Kidgate School.

Louth in the 1830s was a rapidly expanding town. Population increased by nearly 2,000 in the decade to around 8,900 (making Louth the third largest town in the county after Lincoln and Boston) and 425 new houses were built. Many of the houses were small cottages with an average of five people in each. There were two voluntary elementary schools for the poor, under the National Society for the Promotion of the Education of the Poor in the Principles of the Established Church. The National School for boys (1811-12) was in Westgate and that for girls and infants (1833-34) in Enginegate (Broadbank and now a car park). Despite subscriptions, the schools ran a deficit, an indication that many people in the town still needed convincing of the desirability of educating the poor.

Moreover there was a conflict between leading Anglicans and a group of nonconformists, for whom Richard Paddison, the Town Clerk, was the chief spokesman. In a series of pamphlets he upbraided the so-called "Borough Guardian Society" over the rigging of municipal elections, and was particularly vitriolic in attacking the principle of the National Schools in demanding their pupils' exclusive attendance at the Anglican church (St. James and Holy Trinity, then a chapel of ease). In 1840 he quoted incidents when the master of the National School, John Nesbitt, had discharged children because their parents took them to chapel on Sunday, including two daughters of Christopher Scrimshaw, a poor working man living near Monks' Dyke, because they had been taken to the Baptist chapel.

The man to get things moving was John Booth Sharpley, corn and coal merchant at the Riverhead and prominent Wesleyan Methodist who lived in Eastgate House. As Mayor, he convened a public meeting in April 1840, in compliance with a requisition signed by thirty-four influential gentlemen including several Dissenting Ministers. He told the meeting that there were upwards of 1,000 poor children in Louth without means of education, and introduced an agent of the British and Foreign Bible Society to explain how to establish a day school for the children of the poor without distinction of sect or party. The Louth Society for the Education of the Children of the Poor in the principles of the British and Foreign School Society was formed, and application was made to the Borough Council for a site and a grant towards the cost of building.

On 20th April the Council passed the following resolution. "That it is the opinion of the Council that a day-school for the children of the poor in this borough, on the principles of the British and Foreign School Society, is both necessary and desirable, for the following reasons: First, Because there is not any provision whatsoever in Louth for educating the children of the poor in a suitable manner without distinction of sect or party; Secondly, Because for want of such provision a great number of children of both sexes are either not educated at all, or are very improperly educated; and Thirdly, Because the system of the British and Foreign School Society, while it makes use of the whole Bible, imposes no restriction inconsistent with a due regard for the rights of conscience, but opens the door as wide as possible to all denominations of Christians". The Council granted both land for a site and a grant towards building, and annual maintenance expenses of £150.

Application was also made to the Lords of the Treasury for permission to establish a British School, pointing out that the Society promised to "impart in the most efficient manner the principles of all those branches of knowledge that are most useful to the Labourer, the Mechanic and the Artisan." The Government made a grant of £450, the highest for any school in Lincolnshire at the time, towards a final cost of around £1,000. The balance of course was raised by subscriptions.

The piece of land given by the Borough was in Paradise Lane, a close of 2 acres 1 rood 22 perches, occupied as a market garden by Morgan Jones who rented it for £21 a year. Half an acre was divided off by a brick wall 154 yards long, built by William Crow for £127 9s. Clearing the site involved removing 24 apple trees, 19 pear trees, currant and gooseberry bushes and plots of rhubarb and mercury, for which the displaced tenant received £67 15s compensation. The *Lincoln, Rutland & Stamford Mercury*, the main newspaper in the county at the time, enthused that "the intended handsome and spacious building, devoted to so laudable a purpose, will no doubt work a perfect regeneration in this blissful region".

In October 1840, when the school was being erected, it became an issue in the municipal elections. Richard Paddison appealed to burgesses to support the Liberal candidates and so enable the Council to carry out its intention of making a maintenance grant for the British School. This drove the Conservatives to declare their intention, if they obtained a majority on the Council, of preventing the maintenance of the school, and moreover to oust Mr Paddison from the office of Town Clerk. Much of the stiff opposition was organised by the Anglican clergy and laymen, and anonymous pamphleteers from the "establishment camp" produced a stream of invective including the use of epithets like "Men-Trap", "Clap-Trap" and "School-Trap".

According to the *Stamford Mercury* a meeting of Conservatives resolved "1. That this meeting view with disgust the act of the Radicals in the establishing of the British and Foreign School, it being not only an attempt to degrade our ancient institution of the Grammar School, but a dark endeavour to undermine our Holy Episcopal Church. 2. That this meeting regard the education of the children of the poor as

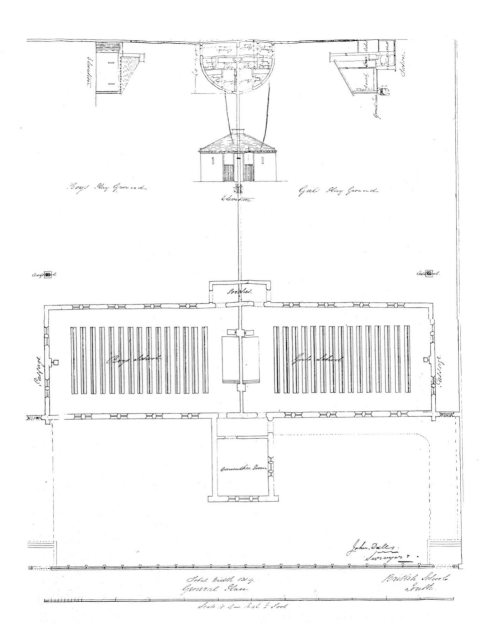

(Lincolnshire Archives Office)

10

The British School in 1844, from William Brown's Panorama of Louth.

The new block built in 1855 (left) and the house which stood at the corner of Cinder Lane.

dangerous to the established order of Society; it invariably raises their minds above labour, thereby rendering them unfit for servants, and consequently encouraging pauperism and crime." These resolutions were denounced as a forgery, but the newspaper asserted that on election day "the Tory subordinates visited every hole and corner in the town; gin-shops vomited forth their inebriated dupes who, mentally shackled, were driven to the poll. Even the sick chamber was not held sacred - one poor man called John Jacklin was taken in a dying state from his bed, wheeled to record his last act in favour of the enemies of the poor, and breathed his last shortly after his return home"!

The Conservatives were defeated, and the Louth British School opened on 1st March 1841 with 160 boys and 150 girls under headmaster James Seller Forster and his wife in charge of the girls. Entrance gates were at either end of the wall facing Kidgate, boys on the left and girls on the right, with paths alongside the front garden where five pear trees had been retained. Doorways in the flanking walls led to separate playgrounds with entrances to the classrooms from porches at the rear. At the far side of the playgrounds was the semi-circular block of privies (often referred to in the school logbooks as "offices") including one each side for the master and mistress and a coal store and ashpit. The projection at the front of the school, with a bell turret, housed the committee room with an outer door on the girls side and access to the two classrooms.

The surveyor who signed the plans was John Dales. He and his brother Benjamin were brickmakers and were probably the builders (John later built the Town Hall in 1854). The bricks were hand-made and burnt in a clamp,, almost certainly in one of the brickpits between Eastgate and Monks' Dyke. The slates and York stone dressings for the windows would have been imported along the Navigation canal. Each classroom was 56ft 4ins by 32ft 9ins, and 18ft 11ins high, with a fireplace against the outside wall at the end of each room. Seating was on raked rows of desk benches facing inwards with curtains between classes. It must have been quite crowded with about 150 children in each room.

As the population of the town continued to increase and the number of children in the school rose to over 450, extra accommodation was required. In 1855 a new block was built, that now facing immediately onto Kidgate (which meant the loss of the five pear trees), joined to the committee room by porch entrances to two classrooms: 18ft 9ins by 24ft and 36ft 6ins by 24ft (with raked seating, for the infants), both 17ft 10ins high. The original bell turret was taken down and a new one built over the central pediment. Because of the slope of the ground construction created a large cellar space under the new classrooms. The bricks were made in Louth, but this time fired in a kiln. At the rear of the original school building a small classroom, 17ft 11ins by 16ft 3ins and only 12ft 11ins high, was built onto the porches and projecting into the playgrounds. The total cost of this work was only £230. A gallery was added to the original girls' room in 1863 at a cost of £3 12s 9d. In 1857 there were 252 boys and 217 girls on the roll, a total of 469 - if they all attended.

Attendance and examination results were key factors in calculating government grants. Parents were required to pay the school pence, 1d or 2d a week (the first quarter of 1866 for example producing £16 5s 10d in the Boys' Department), but voluntary subscriptions were essential for the continuance of the school. In order to secure these the support of leading citizens was required on the Management Committee: patron was the Earl of Yarborough and Vice-Patron the Hon. Charles Tennyson-D'Eyncourt of Bayons Manor; President was J.B. Sharpley, a position he held even (perhaps particularly) when he broke away with the Free Methodists from the Wesleyans and until his death in June 1872, when the school closed on the day of his funeral. The secretary in the 1850s was Revd. J.T. Barker, minister of the Independent Chapel (now the Playhouse Cinema), and the treasurer at that time was James Mawer, manager of W.G. Allinson & Co., wine and spirit merchants in the Cornmarket. There was also a ladies committee.

If the Committee found itself in deficit, as it did by £38 1s 1 1/2d at the annual meeting in 1877, a collection was requested from five dissenting congregations: Independent,

Free Methodist, primitive Methodist and Baptist (Cannon Street and Eastgate), but not from the Wesleyan Methodists because in 1860 they had opened their own day school on Newmarket (now the Playgoers Theatre). Another method of raising funds was a bazaar in the Town Hall; organised by a committee of 13 men and 11 women over a ten-month period, that held on Tuesday, Wednesday and Thursday 3-5 October 1882 raised £409 15s (the equivalent of around £10,000 today!).

Members of the Committee visited the school from time to time, as school governors do now. They were drawn from many walks of life in the town, and some gave talks to the children. When Charles Goodwin Smith, wholesale grocer, tea dealer, soap maker and tallow chandler (26 Upgate) who lived in the White House on Grimsby Road, was President in the 1870s, he instituted the tradition of distributing an orange to each child at Christmas; he also appeared at other times of the year with bags of nuts, but not for any child who had been late for school. His son Saville Smith of 30 Bridge street continued the Christmas orange tradition, and the new President, John Woodrow Dennis, pharmaceutical chemist in Eastgate who lived at Inglethorpe on Newmarket, started in 1895 by presenting every child with two oranges. The tradition appears to have died out before the Great War. Pears, from the school's own trees in what remained of the original orchard, were also distributed to the children in September; in 1874 the crop was so good that each received 30 pears.

Property Matters

THROWING STONES has long been a pre-occupation for small boys. There was no shortage of material before the days of tarmacadam. Not only on Kidgate and Cinder Lane (laid out in 1855), but as late as 1896 HM Inspectors were still drawing attention to the fact that the playgrounds were too stony (despite renovation in 1890). There seems to have been a spate of broken windows from stone-throwing in the 1870s. In April 1870 two boys were punished for breaking a neighbour's window, and again in October. Windows in the school were broken during the holidays, and in May 1875 a reward of £1 was offered for the discovery and conviction of stone-throwers breaking school windows. Four years later the Superintendent of Police was brought in the investigate both broken windows and damage to the school's pear trees. On an earlier occasion, in 1868, the headmaster (David McMichael) decided to pull the pears himself "to prevent the neighbouring roughs pulling them for me".

His successor in the 1870s, James Hargreaves, took the matter of a broken window in the house of Mr Whitney into his own hands. It appears that a number of boys had been loitering nearby and he ordered that each should bring 1/2p to pay for it. Twenty-three boys did, including Richard Goulding, who later gained a scholarship to the Grammar School and went on too be a very respectable citizen of Louth as a printer and bookseller.

Acts of God could also strike windows. During a severe thunderstorm on 24th September 1874 lightning struck the bell turret, scattering stones and bricks over the green and onto the road. One brick crashed through a window of the boys' classroom and "whizzed like a cannon ball past my head". That was headmaster Edward Rogers. In March 1908, when Joseph Trewick was headmaster, one of the school windows fell in, striking him on the head.

On another occasion, in June 1868, the classroom filled with smoke from Charles Ross's pipe factory at 46 Kidgate when he was burning old pipes. David McMichael wrote in the logbook that although he was very fond of tobacco smoke he objected to "inhaling it in that fashion", He sent for "that intelligent and great Superintendent of Police" (William Roberts) who persuaded Mr Ross not to burn old tobacco pipes during school hours. In the school holidays which followed the school was cleaned and painted. Interior decoration usually consisted of whitewashing the walls, although later in the century colour-washing was introduced.

Coke stoves and open fires (suitably guarded) were used to heat the rooms. When the two stoves in the boys' classroom were removed for repair in November 1865, David McMichael note that "unless a school is well warmed, the fingers of the boys become chilled and disabled from performing good writing". As late as 1894, HM Inspector reported that the fire in the main room was insufficient to warm the other end, but it was three years before new "heating apparatus" was installed, and even then an inspector in 1910 found the long stove pipe in the infants' room "objectionable".

Although the town gasworks had opened in 1826, there was no lighting in the school until the 1870s. One day in December 1870 it was dark by 3pm. The master, Edward Rogers, kept on until 3.45 when darkness compelled him to close the school. In 1877 his successor, James Hargreaves, requested the managers to install gas lighting in the boys' room (only?). This was done soon afterwards and each committee member was required to "give or beg" one guinea towards the consequent deficit in the school accounts.

The Boy's School

A key person in the school was the cleaner, particularly perhaps when there was " great fall of soot" when the chimney was being repaired in January 1883; it was so bad that the girls' room had to be closed in the afternoon. Two years earlier the caretaker/cleaner, Mr Brown, had to "be remonstrated with about the dirty state of the school and grounds", but it happened again in 1883 about the untidy schoolroom, badly swept and which "appears never to have been dusted". The school cleaner in 1920 was 40-year old Mrs Jane Wood who was employed 17 1/2 hours a week in the summer and 27 1/2 hours in the winter, and allowed £4 for cleaning materials.

In 1896 the school was using as a workshop (for woodwork) a room over stables at an inn. On the occasion of an inspector's visit in July it was "pervaded by highly objectionable drainage odours that proceeded from the stables". He said that the room was not at all suitable as there was no effective ventilation or heating during the summer months. A year later the school was told that unless a more suitable workshop could be found the grant aid for woodwork would be withdrawn. By 1911 the woodwork classes were being held at the Technical Institute in James Street (built in 1897) on Monday and Wednesday afternoons.

It was not until 1898 that water was laid on to every department in the school, and the following year new "out-offices" with improved closets and urinals were built, for which the school obtained a grant of £48. Doubtless this was the result of continued pressure from HM Inspectors over several years, including the need of a cloakroom for the infants, culminating in the report for 1907 that the need "will no doubt engage the immediate attention of the managers". Cloakrooms for both boys and girls were provided in 1904 by converting the small classroom at the rear of the school, and the girls' closet had an "automatic flush". In 1912 a boy was punished for "dirty ways in the closet - the first case for 15 years; he is a new boy from the country".

When the managers of St. James's school in Enginegate visited in 1906 to look at the sanitary arrangements as they were thinking of making alterations to their own, they

18

"expressed themselves pleased with the Kidgate arrangements". It was not always so. When James Hargreaves took over as headmaster in 1875 he was "worried about the latrines", and there are a number of references to the "offices" needing cleansing. And it was not just the inside and the need to empty the vaults. There was trouble with boys from the street entering the playground in the dinner hour and in the evenings to make marks with crayons on the closet walls (1896), and to carve "very nasty words" on the doors.

Although the number of children on roll declined in the second half of the 19th century (as did the town's population), there were still more than one class in the same room. The average attendance in 1882 was 150 boys and 140 girls. The major need was improved accommodation for the infants, first recommended by the annual meeting of subscribers in 1877, and in 1880 infants were refused admission because of the lack of space (in the block fronting the street), but the work was not done until April 1883. Estimates were obtained from Hurd Hickling (builder and contractor, 138 Eastgate) for brickwork, J.D. McDougald (stonemason and brickmaker of 2 Ramsgate and works off Orme Lane) for stonework, Christopher Adlard (cabinet maker and undertaker, 111 Eastgate) for woodwork, and Martin Colam (plumber and glazier, 105 Eastgate) for glazing, totalling £395, but this had to be reduced to £350 due to shortage of funds.

The work involved taking out an internal wall and there were no infants classes for a week. Three years later a porch was added, but no cloakroom until 1904. The gallery still remained in the main room and was not removed until the Christmas holidays 1906-07. In August 1883, HM Inspector reported that "the infants are well cared for, and now that they have a very good room they should make satisfactory progress in all subjects".

The school became co-educational in June 1898, officially described as Mixed and Infants, with 170 boys and girls and 85 infants in average attendance. The total number of children rose to 275 in 1909, and it became Junior Mixed and Infants from 1915. In 1925 there were still two classes under separate teachers in each of the original classrooms, albeit with wooden partitions installed in 1901.

Following the 1902 Education Act the Kidgate Council School came under the Lindsey County Education Committee from March 1903. The major change in the structure of the school came in 1929 when the elementary schools in Westgate and Enginegate (St James's) and Newmarket (Wesleyan Methodist) closed and Monks' Dyke Senior School opened. This involved demolition of the old committee room, the infants porch and cloakroom, and the former small classroom (then cloakrooms) at the rear of the school, and the construction of a central block joining the 1840 and 1855 buildings with cloakrooms and corridors (one of them within the 1840 building) and first floor staffroom and toilets. Air photographs of May 1930 actually show the work in progress.

The two original classrooms were sub-divided into six rooms and the 1855 block into three classrooms. And a bicycle shed was provided in the playground (repaired with cement in 1918 and now tar sprayed). The toilets, with baffle walls, across the playgrounds (the dividing wall was still there in 1947) were to survive well into the second half of this century. The only signs now of the location of these vital elements of the premises are glazed tiles in the playground walls under the painted murals.

Percy R. Latter took over as headmaster in 1930 (he had been head at the Westgate School for over eleven years, and then lived at 29 George Street), but one item of equipment he never had was the telephone. When Frank Lamming became headmaster in 1947 he applied to the Local Education Authority for one, but was still waiting three years later - on the grounds that there was no canteen in the school. Perhaps there might have been one, and a hall, had the LEA taken advantage of the site of a demolished row of houses immediately east of the school. The Primary Schools Sub-Committee viewed the site in 1935 and again the following year, and then the war intervened.

In 1940 there was grave concern about the lack of provision of air raid shelters for the school. The Mayor of

Louth, Alderman Laurence Lill, said he was not in favour of shelters and declared that "the essence of safety was dispersal". Five shelters were however built during the summer holidays in 1941 among the fruit trees on the strip of land leading to the sports field, with access by two gateways from the playgrounds. The shelters were not removed until 1947. The main gates had iron bars fixed in 1937 "to check the exit of children".

Extensions with toilets and classrooms on the east end of the 1840 block and west end of the 1855 block were built in the 1960s, followed by the hall, and demolition of the house on the corner of Cinder Lane to allow extension of the playground. And the last remaining fruit trees were removed and the former Ropewalk incorporated to enable layout of the sports field.

Kidgate School from the air, late 1960s.

LOUTH BRITISH SCHOOLS.

SPECIAL CERTIFICATE

For Good Attendance.

During the Quarter ending .... Dec. 7th /87 ....

The School was opened .... 127 .... times.

Edward Tendall ....

was present .... 123 .... times.

Geo. Rawson Head Teacher.

22

Teachers and Pupil Teachers

JAMES FORSTER was the first master for the boys, with his wife in charge of the girls. With about 150 children in each room, it must have been a formidable task, although they would have been helped by monitors, and later by pupil teachers. The first pupil teacher of which there is any record was a boy names Hewitt in 1850. By that date Miss Eliza Francis Davis was in charge of the girls. When she and Forster left is not known, but by 1856 the teachers were William Kimm and Miss Georgina Gale, together with ten pupil teachers to instruct 252 boys and 217 girls in five classrooms. The salaries for a quarter totalled £36 19s 5 1/2d: Kimm £11 11s 6d, Miss Gale £7 7s 9d, Miss Shepherd (matron) £4, Miss Morton £2 8s 10d, Miss Read (3rd year pupil teacher) £3 1s 3 1/2d, Mr Marshall £7 2s 11d, Miss Crow 17s and Miss Coleridge 9s 7d.

In 1858 Mary Elizabeth Kimm (daughter of the head), Benjamin Ashton and Frederick Parker became apprenticed as pupil teachers. The following year Kimm brought charges before the managers alleging neglect by Miss Gale of his daughter as a pupil teacher; after hearing her side of it, they found the charges unsubstantiated. Indeed, they resolved that he had "exhibited great animosity against Miss Gale, having tried to secure evidence against her from other pupil teachers, including former pupil teachers then at college, thereby most seriously affecting her influence as mistress of the school". They expressed "great dissatisfaction with his general conduct of the school, chiefly on account of his temper", and his resignation was requested.

23

His successor, David McMichael, who had conducted the British School in Oundle for three years, started on 1st August 1859 at a salary of £80 a year. Miss Gale remained for a further eight years; she went to teach at the Royal Naval Military Schools, Devonport. In 1864 the management committee agreed that the master should receive the school fees, £30 a year from the committee and the government grant payable in respect of the boys' school, out of which he had to pay the salaries of four pupil teachers (Frederick Parker, Benjamin Ashton, Edward Wakelin and Samuel Mawer). Similarly that the mistress should receive the school fees, £10 from the committee and the government grant for the girls, paying three pupil teachers (Sabina Gowshall, Emily Flint and Lucy Gibbons).

Sabina continued into her fifth year (1864) but had to leave because of delicate health. Emily maintained "excellent order with the infants", and went on to Lincoln College. Lucy, despite being reproved for "being so stern and unkind to her class", went on to Stockwell College and visited the school nine years later. There were a number of pupil teachers who visited when they became teachers elsewhere. Frederick Furnish, a pupil teacher 1873-77, visited the following year and again in 1879 and 1881 when he was a teacher at Wisbech. This says much for the affection they had for the school.

When Eliza Croft progressed from being a monitor to pupil teacher for her five-year apprenticeship she was paid £10 a year with an additional £2 10s each succeeding year (she gained a first class scholarship and went to Stockwell College in 1871). However when Alice Wilkinson was apprenticed in 1870 her salary was £8, rising by £2 a year, and Sarah Marshall started on only £4 under a new code in 1872, but then progressed to £11, £13, £15 and £17. Sarah gained her certificate four years later, spending a week in London when taking scholarship examinations.

David McMichael was a keen shot: not only did he take time off, leaving a pupil teacher in charge, to attend battery practice in Grimsby, to go to Saltfleet with the Voluntary Artillery and to take part in the Artillery Carbine prize

Competition, but he also allowed the same pupil teacher, Benjamin Ashton, to attend gun practice in Grimsby. Rather more dangerous was a trapeze which appears to have been in the school; pupil teacher Samuel Mawer fell from the trapeze and was absent on one occasion. On another the master warned two other pupil teachers, Edward Wakelin and Joseph Walliss, against daring acts on the trapeze. Edward was the son of James Wakelin, the town crier, and went on to Borough Road training college in 1866 and to teach at Hartford, visiting the school in 1875. Joseph died later that month (March 1864) "lamented by all his schoolfellows". This did not prevent Joshua Willman, in his first year as a pupil teacher in 1865, injuring his chin in a fall from the trapeze.

McMichael had problems with his pupil teachers in other ways: Mawer was detained for 15 minutes one day for "disorderly movements" (whatever they were), and on another day he "mismanaged his class very much" and also struck pupils. He did, however, complete his four year apprenticeship, and he visited his old school five years later, in 1881. Willman neglected his night work (homework) for a Band of Hope Tea meeting (!), and in his last year (1869) he was seen "smoking a pipe in the public street". Archibald Blair, a second year pupil teacher, was found playing with a ball in the classroom, having upset an inkstand and splashed ink on the walls. More serious was the case of Edward Cash: having been left in charge of the boys' playground, he was found "upon the boundary wall spitting on some boys"; later that year (1866) his indentures were cancelled. However, the value of pupil teachers was shown in the inspector's report in February 1866: "I do not think this school can be properly disciplined with less than four pupil teachers".

Miss Gale resigned at the end of the spring term 1867 and entered in the logbook "liberated on Lady Day"! Her successor, Miss Jane Gibson, only stayed a year, but Miss Mary Ann Tiley stayed for fifteen years until 1883 when she got married. She was successful and well liked. After only two years the management committee resolved that "Miss Tiley be presented with a donation of £10 as an expression of their

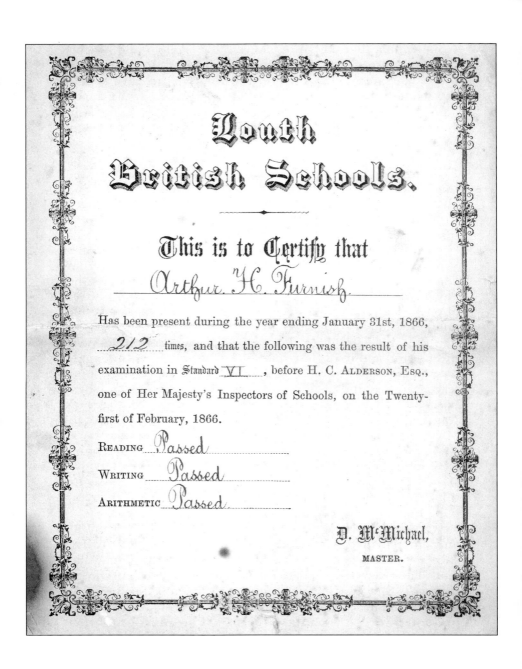

Louth
British Schools.

This is to Certify that

Arthur H. Furnish

Has been present during the year ending January 31st, 1866,

_212_ times, and that the following was the result of his

examination in Standard VI , before H. C. ALDERSON, Esq.,

one of Her Majesty's Inspectors of Schools, on the Twenty-

first of February, 1866.

READING _Passed_

WRITING _Passed_

ARITHMETIC _Passed_

D. McMichael,
MASTER.

satisfaction at the increase in scholars and the manner in which she has discharged her duties". A similar donation was made in at least five succeeding years. In 1881 the children (223 of them present for the occasion) and pupil teachers presented her with a silver locket and the following year a silver necklet to go with it, and when she left to marry in 1883 the pupil teachers gave her a floral portrait album. She had lived at 2 George Street.

Pupil teachers who served under Miss Tiley included Lavinia Kime (who started in 1869 and returned ten years later as an assistant), Annie Huddlestone (she returned as a certificated teacher with the infants in 1883), Lucy Garnett (she left after four years to become a groom), Clara Plaskett (she went on to become an assistant teacher in Halifax) and later her sister Edith, Charlotte Crofts (she gained a 2nd class in the Queen's scholarship, which meant an extra £2 in government grant when she became an assistant at Killingholme), Emily Cotton, Bertha Topham, and Fanny Pridmore (a fourth year pupil teacher from Leicester on £18 a year). She also had Miss Elvina Robinson as assistant mistress in 1879 at £35 a year. Ellen Colbeck started her pupil teaching in 1875 (she taught the infants) and went on to become an assistant at £35 in the first year and £40 in the second; when she left to get married in 1882 the chairman of the managers, C.G. Smith, presented her with half a dozen electric (electro-plated) forks, breakfast cruet and butter dish and knife.

The infants were also under the charge of Miss Tiley, and numbers became such that in 1880 she had to refuse entry to any more because of the lack of space. Under a new government code the school was required to provide eight square feet for every child in average attendance. It is no surprise that when she left in 1883 to run her own private ladies school at 44 Westgate, she was replaced by two teachers - Miss Sarah Jane Paull, a certificated teacher from Cornwall at £50 a year (plus part of the government grant for infants) for the girls, and Miss Ada Kate Knowles, a certificated teacher from the Wesleyan school in Lowestoft at £50 a year for the infants. That year there was an average attendance of 150 boys and 140 girls, and the infants' schoolroom had been improved.

When Edward Rogers had been appointed master in September 1869, he received the fees - 2d a week from those parents who could afford it (about £50 a year), a stipend of £40 and half (about £20) of the government grant. One of his pupil teachers was George Croft who would appear to have been less than satisfactory: "all his home lessons wrong, a very common occurrence". He was "wrecked on Pons Asinorum", wrote Rogers, but "after explaining it with great care, he was as wise as ever". (Pons Asinorum, meaning bridge of asses, was a humorous name for the fifth theorem of Euclid, from the difficulty which beginners or dull-witted persons found in "getting over" or mastering it.) The next month his Euclid was still "unsatisfactory", and a few weeks later he was caught getting into the schoolroom through a window at dinner time. He did however complete his apprenticeship, and was asked to take charge of the school when Rogers was in London sitting his BA examination. He went on to teach in Nottingham, and visited the school again two years later.

The other pupil teacher, Joseph George Smith, left after two years as "he thought teaching would be too arduous, and he had a notion of obtaining a clerkship in Hull". Rogers described him as "a useful and intelligent youth". When the school put an advertisement in the local newspaper for a replacement, three replies were from former scholars. But after six years as master, the secretary had to write to Rogers that "having taken into consideration the dissatisfaction existing among the subscribers to the school and the parents of the scholars", it was felt to be in the best interests of the school to give him three months notice. He left in May 1876 and was succeeded by James Hargreaves.

As part of their apprenticeship the pupil teachers had extra lessons from the master, at 6am (!) and after school, as well as homework. During his thirteen years as master, Hargreaves (he lived at 3 Clarence Terrace) had a timetable for the pupil teachers: Monday - arithmetic and geometry; mapping. Tuesday - algebra and geography; history.

Wednesday - grammar; history. Thursday - arithmetic; geometry. Friday - algebra and geometry; history. They took their examinations with other pupil teachers in the town at the National School in Westgate. A government grant was paid in respect of pupil teachers, of which two-thirds went to the master and mistress, and a third to the pupil teachers themselves. Charles Wells was already a pupil teacher when Hargreaves became head. William White was off for some time in 1877 when he broke his leg, Frank Hickling, probably the son of the builder who did the work on the school, started as a paid monitor, progressing from £8 to £13, £18 and £22 a year (he was absent on one occasion following "an accident with a horse on Mablethorpe sands"), and Ernest Coppin advanced in the same way.

The year that Hargreaves took over (1876) saw the opening of St. Michael's school on Church Street (designed by James Fowler and demolished in 1981) and some pupils transferred to it. Other competition came from the National Schools in Westgate and Enginegate, the Wesleyan School on Newmarket (opened 1869, now the Playgoers Theatre) and Holy Trinity Parochial Schools (1865, enlarged 1879, later Eastfield Road and now part of the North Lincolnshire College). At the time of the 1870 Education Act the Borough Council decided to save itself the trouble and expense of appointing a School Board as it considered there were sufficient places available in elementary schools in the town, although the census figures the following year hardly left room for complacency. By the 1880s there were some 2,400 places available in all Louth schools, but the average attendance in the last two decades of the century seldom exceeded 1,500, even though the Borough Council had made a bye-law in 1878 making school attendance compulsory between the ages of 5 and 13. However in those twenty years the population of the town contracted by 1,200. The numbers on roll at the British School tended to reflect this trend, and when Hargreaves left in 1889 to take over the commercial school on Northgate (at the corner of Broadbank, now demolished and the site is a block of flats) the number of children totalled 273 - 93 boys, 115 girls and 65 infants.

We know that the girls were divided into six Standards; the first three (with about 25 in each) were taken by pupil teachers and the others by the mistress (in 1887 there were only five girls in Standard VI). Standard I was taken by Emily Colam (probably the daughter of the plumber and glazier who did work on the school, and she had already sat an examination at the Royal College of Music), the "only teacher who can be held responsible for a class", with monitor Lucy Smith for the slower ones. Standard II was taken by Rachel Stokes (she started 1886), and Standard III by Emily Thompson who had started with the infants but failed her certificate exam in 1891 and left the following year. Others did better: Ella Elsom won first prize in a national competition in 1890 and went on to gain a 1st class Queen's scholarship in 1895, and Ann Millhouse who also won a certificate of merit in the national competition. Other pupil teachers for the girls included Lucy Colam, Frances Amelia Smith, Alice Dring and Clara Vickers. One day in March 1894, when the children were in the playground, Mrs. Emerson of 7 Brocklebank's Yard entered the girls' classroom and assaulted one of those junior teachers.

Although Emma Neal had been accepted as a pupil teacher for the infants in 1890, she was unable to continue "owing to the precarious nature of her mother's health". The logbook for the Infants Department records that the weather was very stormy on Tuesday 2nd and Wednesday 3rd March 1896, and as there were less than twenty children present they were sent home for the rest of the week. The pupil teachers did not escape however, and had extra instruction for three hours each morning. In the autumn term 1894 there was a gap between infants teachers Miss Metcalfe and Miss Burton, and Alice Holland, then in her final year as a pupil teacher, took charge; when she left she was presented with a volume of Tennyson's poems.

After Hargreaves the next master, George Rawson, resigned after little more than a year, and his successor, John Edward Cheese (he lived at 18 George Street) only stayed four years. Meanwhile Miss Paull and Miss Knowles had been replaced by Miss Annie Browning (girls) and Miss Charlotte

Metcalfe (infants), and they in turn by Miss Margaret Rait Knox (two years) and Miss Emily Burton (three years), all within the space of five years, and staffing did not stabilise until the late 1890s.

Pupil teachers under Rawson were George Larder and William Wheatcroft. Miss Burton brought some rapid improvement in discipline and method to the Infants Department when she arrived in 1895, but with the difficulties over a mistress for the girls, discipline there was weak, and "most of the work appears to be wanting in neatness" an inspector reported. He also commented that "preparation for the school concert should not interfere with the general working of the school".

Matters improved generally under the stable headship of Joseph Trewick from December 1894, and particularly with the appointment in 1899 of Miss Lucy Gray for the girls and of Mrs Margaret Brocklebank for the infants, both certificated. Trewick lived first at 17 George Street and later at Delaval House in Kidgate, and received a salary increase of £40 in 1901, and Mrs Brocklebank £25; her husband Arthur was a teacher of music and they lived at 2 Quarry Terrace. All their four children did well in the school: Roy was placed first in the entrance scholarship to the Grammar School, Raymond became a monitor and then a pupil teacher, Margaret progressed from pupil teacher to assistant to her mother for seven years to 1905, and Maud gained a pupil teacher scholarship in 1905.

The boys and girls departments had been amalgamated in June 1898, and in September the following year it was noted that the boys and girls were "doing good work". The pupil teachers then were George Dennis, Charles Donner, Anne Faulds and Jessie Rowe, all later completing their apprenticeships. Although Donner was once sent home for a week "for insubordination to Miss Gray", he became an assistant at Whitstable; Dennis gained a 2nd class Queen's scholarship and became assistant in a London school; Anne Faulds also gained a 2nd class but stayed on as an assistant until she married a soldier "proceeding to the front" in 1915; and Jessie Rowe became an assistant at Heywood, Lancashire.

Good Attenders. Louth British Boys. July 1897.
(see page 54). Headmaster Joseph Trewick with his dog.

SPECIAL CERTIFICATE

FOR GOOD ATTENDANCE

During the Quarter ending May 28th '98

the School was opened 119 times

Edward Birdsall

was present One hundred & fifteen times.

Thos. S. Rawson HEAD TEACHER.

33

Staffing distribution in 1900 was: Standard I Jessie Rowe, Standard II Charles Donner, Standard III Miss Gray, and Standard IV to VII Mr Trewick with the help of Albert Coppin (he went on to Reading University College in 1903) for Standard IV and John Milson for Standard V. With only four classrooms it still meant more than one class in a room , and in 1901 a grant of £24 was received towards the construction of partitions. The infants of course had their own classroom.

The name of the school changed over the years, starting as the British School, then referred to as the Louth British Schools after the provision of separate accommodation for the infants. It was also known as the British and Undenominational School or Louth Undenominational School (1917) and again as Louth British Schools (1918), the latter two on school reports - but they may have been using up old stock. After the 1902 Education Act it was the Kidgate Mixed and Infants School until changes in the 1920s under Lindsey County Council.

When the Pupil Teacher Centre opened in January 1904 at the Technical School, the pupil teachers were required to attend there two days one week and three days the next, and this necessitated alterations in the timetable. Then in 1906 the school received a letter from the Board of Education requiring strengthening of the adult staff, otherwise the Board would be "unable to sanction under Article 8 of the Pupil Teacher Regulations the employment of the present large number of pupil teachers". At that time there were 190 boys and girls and 85 infants attending, Lindsey County Council having directed in 1905 that no more children under 5 years could be admitted.

The school therefore had to follow this directive and reduce the number of pupil teachers. Mrs Trewick, wife of the head and a certificated teacher, did some supply teaching, Emily Smith (pupil teacher 1902-04) returned as a certificated teacher until at least 1922 (in March 1917 she took charge of the school at Welton le Wold for two weeks), former pupil teacher Ethel Skinn became an assistant (to 1907), Florence Grantham was an uncertificated teacher for the infants, and Edwin B. Markham joined the staff as a certificated teacher.

Ethel Hutchinson (she started as a monitor and passed the London Matriculation), William Sylvester, Hilda Marsh (1909-11) and Hilda Lill (she returned as an infants teacher in 1918-19 following the resignation of Mrs Brocklebank after 20 years service) all gained pupil teacher scholarships. Assistants for the Infants Department included Hilda M. Burton (1903-09), Miss Mary Knight (from Chapman Street Infants, Grimsby) and Miss L.A. Wilyman who went on to be in charge of the infants at Eastfield Road school.

Other pupil teachers through to the 1920s it has been possible to trace through the logbooks were Edith Walker (1905-07; she "promises to be a good and painstaking teacher"), Marion Gell (1912-14; she went to Lincoln Training College and was in the school as an unqualified teacher in 1920), Ivy Hardcastle, Kitty Smith, Clarice Birkett, Ruth Baines, Mable Staples, Grace Kirkham, Ida Lowry, Edith Bontoft (she later became a teacher in the re-organised school), Florence

Joseph Trewick and his staff c.1906.

35

Hundleby, Marjorie Moody, Elsie Maughan, Edith Rawlings, Dorothy Hammond (1927), Winnie Helmsley, and Ethel Rawlings (1927).

A visitor to the school in June 1919 was Mrs Sarah Johnson, nee Paull, a teacher there in 1883-86. When Mrs. Brocklebank resigned in 1918 she was presented with a gold brooch and handbag, and when Miss Gray left after 27 years "faithful and efficient service" in 1925 to marry a Mr. Gray, the teachers and children gave her a case of cutlery. Miss Ethel E. Darnell was in charge of the infants for three years (1919-22), succeeded by Miss Edith M. Sawyer and later (c. 1926) by Miss Jane Burdett.

The same term Miss Gray left, Joseph Trewick (who had also been head of the Municipal Technical College from 1919), "beloved headmaster of this school for 31 years", died on the afternoon of Wednesday 9th December. Mr Edward Wright took temporary charge, followed in January by Mr. R.J. Ogden (he had just retired as head of the Wesleyan Day School in Horncastle) and Mr. J.F. Beetlestone (he was joint secretary of the Louth Naturalists', Antiquarian & Literary Society and lived at Northfield, Brackenborough Road). Mr. Trewick's death heralded a difficult time for the school, with also a re-organisation scheme for Louth schools. Kidgate became a Council Senior Mixed School and Mr. William Forster from Eastfield Road school took charge in April 1926, bringing three teachers with him, Miss Haynes, Miss Eaton and Miss Cook, while Miss Butterwick transferred to the Enginegate Girls School.

Moreover, the school was arranged in classes according to the children's ability, and Mr. Forster noted that "the standard of work was much below what it should be" and that "due allowance should be made in assessing the work of teachers at the end of term". It was a time of much change: Mr. Leslie R.D. Beck only stayed six months, Mrs. Broughton and Mr. Gwilliam left, and in September Mr. David A. Davies, Mr. Ronald P. Lovatt and Miss Marjorie Ayres joined the staff, Mrs. F.M. Towle was a supply teacher and Miss Elsie Giddings joined the staff in July 1927.

The School Report

SURVIVAL of the school in its early years, and certainly until elementary education became free in 1891, depended on a favourable report from HM Inspector. His recommendations determined the level of government grant: it was payment by results. The grant was received in April, which was also the beginning of the school year as it had opened in March. Members of the management committee would also visit from time to time, both to check that the teachers were doing a good job and to lend encouragement. At the end of the summer term there would be a public examination before the President of the committee. The school also had an annual visit from an agent of the British & Foreign School Society.

The first mention in the logbook (1863) was that Arithmetic in B division was uncertain, that a new system was being introduced - where a boy checks and proves his own work, and that there was a weekly arithmetic exam. In spelling exams the teachers had to be vigilant to prevent copying and in 1865 the inspector reported that in Standard IV the spelling was not accurate enough. The younger children at that time were using moveable slates. The inspector noted that reading in the lower classes was not "clear, loud or accurate enough". By 1866 the inspector reported that "discipline was more complete than I had ever found it", but the girls did not "speak out in answering clearly and audibly" (they used Chambers Standard Readers).

New examination forms were introduced in 1868, and the headmaster, David McMichael, complained that they were "decidedly more difficult to fill up and the changes are very trying to teachers" (shades of things to come). The inspection however was satisfactory in both instruction and discipline, and of the 132 children entered for the three Rs - Reading Writing and Arithmetic, there were only 23 failures, those in reading "caused by low indistinct manner of utterance". The resulting grant totalling £81 12s 6d (attendances £25 4s, exams £45 1s 4d, Infants £2 5s 6d, extra subjects £6 13s 4d, and for children above the 6th Standard, that is over 13 years of age, £2 8s).

On the matter of discipline, one amusing incident was recorded. In October 1865 the headmaster had left the school for part of the day in the care of pupil teachers. A boy named Flemming, admitted about ten days previously, made a great deal of noise and neither the pupil teachers nor Miss Gale (girls' mistress) were able to govern him and they sent him home. "He left the room but remained in front of the school shouting and threatening the teachers to the insane delight of the respectable and other females in the neighbourhood". The logbook for the next day merely says "Punish Flemming" (with the cane of course).

It is not clear what the extra subjects were, but we know that in the 1860s the girls did needlework and the boys geometrical drawing, they studied geography, including lessons on the geography of Lincolnshire, on Russia, and on rail communication with London and a voyage to Barnsley to fetch coal (but the girls had "no real grasp of geography"), and history including a lesson on the reign of Queen Victoria. Singing was important (songs such as "Come, boys, be merry" and "Paddle my own canoe" were taught, and in January 1865 the school performed at an evening exhibition in the Town Hall), as was drill (on one occasion the boys performed badly and were detained to 5.10 p.m. for further practice), but there was a special lesson on silk ribbon weaving, and reference to the receipt of a "galvanic battery" from the Science & Art Department implies some simple physics for the upper standards.

Not all children used slates of course, but it was not until 1902 that they were finally discarded, and a recipe used for making ink was: mix 6oz purified sulphate of iron, 2oz powdered nut galls and 2oz powdered gum arabic; use a teaspoonful of powder to one pint of cold soft rainwater; ready in 12 hours.

There was play as well as work. The school had a Maypole, there was a great bonfire in the playground after school on November 5th, the boys went swimming and took part in a match in the river (one of the mill ponds?) - "have used the baths much this season (1866) much to the benefit of the boys", and they were taken to play football in Hubbard's Hills. The children were also taken out of school to Miss Montague's Mesmeric Establishment, and to an exhibition of marionettes at the Town Hall.

The first inspection of the 1870s showed the problems of the "payment by results" system. "The older scholars show ignorance in the meaning of words in reading, for example fertile, settlement, recant, infamous, explored. Another time I shall recommend a reduction of grant on this ground". The next year however the school was in a "pretty fair state of efficiency". Over the next few years the inspector commented on writing "not sufficiently neat, even on slates, of course it would be worse on paper", arithmetic "requires particular attention", algebra and geometry "failures", singing and recitation "good", poetry "fairly mastered", grammar "moderate", and reading "pretty good".

In 1872 the headmaster, Edward Rogers, tried to improve examination standards in arithmetic by using Gill's Cards for Standard II, but "the result was ridiculous. Scarcely any boys worked the sums satisfactorily, and the marvel would be if any boys of 8 were generally able to work these sums. Shall get Jarrold's Cards which I believe are better adapted to school work" (which he did). He was also critical of the length of dictation, covering half a page of foolscap with only two mistakes allowed, and also said that the boys wrote too fast for improvement. Just what effect all this had on the grant is not

This is to Certify

THAT

Richard Ball

was examined by

H. M. Inspector

and passed in the sixth standard on

June 18 90

Signed Charles Mansen

Head Master

known, but in 1875 it was £80, a reduction of £7 8s on the previous year.

From November 1877 the new headmaster, James Hargreaves, took a special reading class from 5.15 to 6pm. A dozen of the best boys provided themselves with Scott's "Ivanhoe", which they finished in April the next year. "My aim", he wrote, "is to give them a taste for reading". Geography was still not a strong subject for the girls ("feeble" according to the inspector), despite acquisition of a dozen wall maps including two of Lincolnshire, the British Isles and the World from Stanfords (they are still suppliers in Long Acre, London).

The bright spot was drawing, with examinations in geometrical, freehand and model drawing. In 1874 the girls obtained 28 first grades, and 41 in 1878, and the results for the boys were prizes for George Elmer and Albert Tatam and certificates of proficiency for Jesse Gresswell, Freeman Smith and Henry Blanchard (1876), and Excellent (Robert Appleby and Thomas Marshall) with nine proficient, 48 satisfactory and only four failures (1880; the drawing grant that year was £3 17s 9d for the boys and £3 14s 3d for the girls). This could not be said of grammar and geography in 1880 when the examination papers were "so indifferent" that no grant could be recommended. Improvement was rapid: "Geography answers correctly and readily" (1881).

During the decade there was a lesson on the ostrich and a visit to an exhibition of English snakes, but the main concern was with children being late for school. The logbook records of James Hargreaves are worth quoting in full:

1877 June 8:   "Just after opening the school this afternoon the father of a boy called Arthur Johnson visited the school. This boy passed the third standard on 8 February 1876 in all subjects. On February 5 and 6 this year he passed fourth standard in all subjects. His age when he passed the fourth standard was 11 yrs 2 months. He has given me much trouble for a long time by coming late but I have never punished him in any way in any single instance when he has brought a note from home stating the cause of being late. This morning he

41

came late without a note and I chastised him. The father said he had come to see about his lad being caned for coming late. The matter was explained to him - when he said he was sure the managers of the school did not know that I was so particular about lads being in time, but he would see them. If his lad could not be allowed to come a few minutes late, he would take him away. It was explained that on no account could an exception be made in his case. No fault was found in his threat that he would see the managers, neither was fault found with his decision to take his son away because he found the discipline too hot for him, but when he began to use abusive language and talk about things foreign to the question at issue, I felt I had no alternative but to order him off the premises, which I did".

This entry is countersigned by Rev. E. Eastwick, a nonconformist minister and manager.

1878 April 5 (Friday): "Mrs Gow, Mrs Larder and Mrs Thompson came to see me in school to see if they could arrange with me to allow their boys to come in a little late as it was not the fault of the boys but their mothers' fault. I refused to discuss the question with them but gave them clearly to understand that I would allow no such thing. They all went away vexed saying they could have to take them to another school".

April 8 (Monday):   "Joshua Larder, John Gow and George Thompson all in good time today!"

The previous month the following Circular to Parents was approved by the school managers to be read to parents when they apply for the admission of their child; it does much to explain the system operating then.

"Parents and others who apply for the admission of children to these schools should consider whether they can comply with the requirements of those who pay for the education given at these schools. The funds are supplied partly by the State and paid out of the Parliamentary fund administered by the Education Department and partly from friends of religious non-sectarian education. The State requires that before any child is examined for the purpose of a grant, such child must have attended at least 250 times during the school year and that he must be present when the inspector makes his annual visit to the school, or no grant will be paid on his behalf.

The managers require that the parents conform to the following rules. The prizes given by the managers at midsummer are awarded to those children who attain the highest number of marks and marks are given every time the school is open to scholars, who are present at 9 o'clock and half past one.

The State undertakes to pay the school fees of those children who before they are 11 years of age pass the fourth standard and have attended 350 times or more in each of two years. Parents who comply with the above and thus secure the well-being of the school are at the same time promoting the highest interests of their children".

In July 1878 Alfred Snowden was 7 yrs 10 months old and had been absent from school for a month. The schools attendance officer, William Keith (of 39 James Street) finally caught up with him, took him to the Town Hall where he remained all night (in a cell?) and brought him to the school. The following day his mother "whipped him to school", but he left at noon and played truant in the afternoon! Unfortunately we don't know what happened next.

The case of Charles Walmesly was different. His mother called to see Hargreaves - "She evidently thought of dictating to me as to what class Charles should be put in - classification of boys must be left to me". Under the regulations which came in after education became compulsory in 1880, each child had a School Book; this was kept by the teacher, attendances marked and standards passed entered, and it was given to the child on leaving or moving to another school.

Louth Undenominational Schools.

HEADMASTER :—JOS. TREWICK., A.C.P.

Scholar's Report for Term ending Christmas 1917

Name of Scholar......Olive Kirk...................... Standard...Class I (a)

Number of Scholars in class.........25........ Scholar's number in order of merit.........5.........

Subject.	Possible marks.	Marks obtained.	Remarks.
Reading	100		
Composition	100		
Handwriting	100		
Written } Arithmetic Mental }	100		
	100		
Geography	100		
English	100		
History	100		
Recitation	100		
Drawing (boys)	100		
Needlework (girls)	100		
Hygiene	100		
Algebra	100		
Sculpture			
Woodwork			
Gen. Total Knowledge			

Possible marks for Term.....1300.....

Actual marks for Term....107.5.

Number of lessons missed
on account of absence...........

Number of times school has been open......1114....

Number of times present......1111....

Number of times absent.........2.......

Conduct.........................Excellent........................

Signed

J. Trewick

Headmaster.

44

Louth Undenominational Schools.

HEADMASTER :—JOS. TREWICK., A.C.P.

Scholar's Report for Term ending ___Christmas___ 1917

Name of Scholar......*Alec Davey*...................... Standard......*Class I(a)*

Number of Scholars in class............25......... Scholar's number in order of merit..........................

Subject.	Possible marks.	Marks obtained.	Remarks.
Reading	100	88	
Composition	100	70	
Handwriting	100	81	
Written } Arithmetic	100	98	
Mental }	100	90	
Geography	100	70	
English	100	73	
History	100	70	
Recitation	100	50	
Drawing *(boys)*	100	71	
Needlework *(girls)*	100	—	
Hygiene	100	64	
Algebra	100	24	
Scripture		G,	
& Woodwork		78	
Gen. Knowledge Total		75	

Possible marks for Term......1300...

Number of times school has been open..........1144....

Number of times present..........111....

Conduct..................*Very Good*........................

Actual marks for Term ...1002..

Number of lessons missed
on account of absence........0.......

Number of times absent........0.....

Signed

J. Trewick

Headmaster.

45

The next decade - the 1880s - saw the Infants recorded as a separate department under Miss Ada Knowles. Their order and singing was "good" and they were "nicely taught". Equipment acquired included more slates from the boys' department, bead wires "to teach numeration", 250 small cubes and three dozen tin saucers, pencils, chalk, foolscap paper, a T-square and four dozen thimbles, together with "a modulator and two signals" (for what purpose is not recorded). At their annual inspection in 1886 they sang, recited, marched and answered questions on lessons about candles, the moon, and a blacksmith. They also had a treat when they went to the Sunday Schoolroom in Cannon Street (now the Playhouse) where they had a tea, gave recitations and sang, with a magic lantern show by William Goodall (gardener of Gospelgate).

For the girls the inspector reported that their needlework was good (they won prizes at the school exhibition), singing and drill good, spelling and arithmetic weak, but geography only fair "and for this the grant was barely earned" (1882). The following year he complained that the style of handwriting was affected by the desks being too narrow, with those behind being raised, and that a supply of ruled slates was required; for the writing exam later in the year the upper standard were taught a "pointed hand". In 1884 the girls were "very boisterous in their movements", and Fanny Robinson "behaved very naughtily - sulked and said her recitation indistinctly".

Among the six girls who received prizes for regular attendance in 1886 was Gertrude Goulding (younger sister of Richard who had gone to the Grammar School), and there were 22 certificates of good attendance (and 42 in 1887). The school managers also presented illuminated certificates to children passing three subjects in the government examination. However in 1887, according to the Town Clerk, Thomas Falkner Allison, the British School attendance was the most unsatisfactory in the town (was it worse than the average annual attendance ten years before - boys 87 out of 120 (72.5%) and girls 125 of 200 or 62.5%?). Certainly the teachers were complaining about the laxity of the attendance committee and their officer, Mr Keith, although in 1888 the average attendance of the girls was 124 of 146 (85%). Six years later the headteachers of the Louth schools were again discussing with the Town Clerk ways of improving the methods of the schools attendance officer.

After successes in drawing, it must have been disappointing that under new rules in 1887 the subject could not be taken by the girls unless the timetable provided for the teaching of cookery. Drawing was therefore discontinued and needlework or the weakest subject substituted. However, by 1890 the girls were being examined in Domestic Economy, and the boys had continued with drawing, helping towards a grant of £74 for the school. There is also reference in the boys' department logbook to an evening school which had an average attendance of 41.3, but no indication of the subjects. All this would have been of no concern to three girls in Class I - Alice Hill, Ada Butters and Sarah Lancaster - who were detained till 5.30 p.m. for "disobedience and rude behaviour" and generating insubordination in the rest of the class. Three days later Ada Butters and Fanny Broughton were caned for "wilful disobedience".

In October 1891 the new headmaster, Edward Cheese, met with the management committee, parents and subscribers to discuss the effect of the Free Education Act on the finances of the school, and to ask for subscriptions to the School Fund. The next month he complained that there were several boys in Standard I "who cannot read as well now as they should have done in the Infants". Two years before six girls in Standard I had to be returned to the Infants because they were so backward. And in the Infants a pupil teacher taught history and geography "by the bad method of learning pieces by rote from the textbooks" (echoes of the capes and bays approach). School hours were changed for the infants in the winter, closing the register at 1.55 and lessons to 3.30 with no break, thus "embracing the required 1 1/2 hours".

The boys had started learning shorthand in 1892, but by the end of the year Mr. Cheese reported to the inspector that it would have to be omitted from the timetable because of the small number in the class and the difficulty of the subject. It was replaced by "class subjects, drill and the metric system". Meanwhile the girls' department received a glowing report from the inspector: "Better and more even work than before. Reading, spelling and writing deserve special praise. Drill very good". (The upper standard had recently started scarf drill). The girls in the upper standards were given a lecture on Alcohol by Titus Topham (miller) with one on Temperance the following year, and in 1901 forty boys in the upper classes joined the Anti-Cigarette League, promising not to smoke before they were 21. At the annual prize distribution by J.W. Goulding (stationer and father of Richard and Gertrude) in July 1894, the headmaster showed views of Stately Homes of England by "limelight lantern".

Joseph Trewick, early 1920's

The Trewick Years

KIDGATE's longest serving headmaster, Joseph Trewick (from Cornwall), took up his appointment on Friday 7th December 1894, his predecessor having only resigned on Monday 12th November. He died still in post, in his 50s, almost exactly 31 years later, on 9 December 1925. He was an Associate of the College of Preceptors (ACP) and his wife was a certificated teacher. They had two children born in Louth, Doris Mary and John Arthur, and he proudly recorded their educational progress in his school logbooks: Doris went to Stockwell College in 1915 and then to St. Andrew's University, graduating as LLA in 1922, the same year as her brother graduated in medicine and surgery, MB and ChB, at Leeds (having been awarded a Lindsey Senior Scholarship from Louth Grammar School in 1916).

Trewick saw the school successfully through the transition to a mixed school (1898) and County Council control (1903), and through the traumas of the Great War, he introduced school photographs (1897), an annual sports afternoon (1900), gardening to the timetable (1918), printed school reports, he improved the standards of teaching and increased the number of scholarships awarded. Some of the annual inspector's reports and other logbook entries tell the story.

1895 June (Girls): "Attention must be paid to slate cleaning or the Department grant may be lost". Two weeks later slate cleaning "apparatus" was introduced.

August (Boys): "The school has maintained its old character for good work".

1896 February (Girls): Following a visit without notice - "Discipline very weak, neatness in work poor, few able to say the poetry chosen for recitation".

July (Girls): "The school is in fair condition, but the report of the visit in the winter was so unfavourable that unless work is improved the rate of payment will be reduced".

1899 February: Infants began using paper instead of slates.

1900 July: Highest grants awarded in all subjects. "The school is in capital condition, and the girls have been brought up to the level of the boys".

1901 May (Infants): "Children nicely taught". (Eight years before less than half the children in Class I passed the 3Rs exam)

1902 April (Infants): "School satisfactorily taught but irregular answering should be checked". ("Indiscriminate chorus answering must be reduced" - 1905)

1904 July (Infants): "Continue to be suitably taught".

1905 September: "Older children have a practical working acquaintance with the principles of the metric system".

1910 October (Infants): "Desks are poor and the little ones sit on forms without backs doing needlework". By December, 24 new dual desks had been supplied by the County Council (and eight more in 1912).

1910 September: The headmaster was congratulated on his excellent work and results.

1911 January: The boys start woodwork at the Technical School.

1914 March: An excellent report on the operation of the school (this despite only having an allowance for the year of £32 14s 6d for exercise books, £2 for apparatus and £2 for furniture, but the school got its first sewing machine for the girls in 1916).

1921 February: "The children work steadily and for the most part give the impression of being interested in the work".

The last report of Trewick's headship (1925) is a fine testimonial to his achievements. It noted that Religious Knowledge was excellent in Standard VI, and that the tone and discipline leave nothing to be desired. It refers to "the first class profit from the direct personal influence of the Head Teacher; the pupils show commendable interest in and concentration on their work, but adequate arrangements are yet to be made for the benefit of the more advanced and capable children who appear to mark time when required to share the instruction addressed collectively to the group as a whole". (The last point was really a reflection of the inadequacy of the accommodation, and it was sad that Trewick did not live to see the rebuilt school and classrooms which were, even then, being planned). "The children of Standards V and VI can express themselves with good effect in written English, there is a reasonable degree of accuracy in Arithmetic, and Geography stresses information and description; Singing is carefully taught, but regrets there is no piano available".

It seems that Trewick was keen to encourage sporting and other activities. Bar-bell Drill was introduced in 1895, and in June 1910 the upper standard girls "commenced with the organised game Net-Ball" - in the playground as the school was still waiting to hear about the provision of a playing field. In

Back row (L-R): *F Maudron, Handley, Jarvis, Beard, Wilkinson, Beard, Goodall, D Maudron.*
Front row: *Perfect, Vickers, F Hosier, Barker, Smith, Langley, Hall, Tomlinson, Smalley.*

1908

Louth British Mixed, Group 2

1911

July 1904 several of the top class boys went to camp for a week, and in September 1918 he took the boys brambling but the result did not "justify the loss of half a day's lessons". Then in June 1919 the school commenced organised games when Standards IV to VII were taken to Louth cricket field and the children were provided with "6 small balls, 2 cricket balls, 3 large balls, 3 footballs, 2 wickets (sets presumably) and one set of bails, 2 cricket bats, 2 pairs of netball posts and nets; friends provided the braids and parents the shoes". The next February Captain Grenfell visited the school to lecture on Organised Games, and in March two drill teams were successful in the drill section of the Louth Eisteddfod. Earlier the County Council Drill Instructress, Miss E.C. Terry, pronounced herself "pleased with the deep breathing". From 1923, at 3 o'clock on Thursday afternoons the children marched to the field for games. And in January 1925 Trewick organised a double session of teaching to allow most of the school to go to the football match between Louth and Spilsby Policemen when the proceeds were for the hospital.

The same month the school performed Babes in the Wood, one of the pageant scenes in the Town Hall in aid of the Waifs and Strays. Earlier, in 1923, the whole school visited a Missionary Exhibition in the Town Hall which was "most interesting and informative with each country lectured upon by a missionary who had lived there", and in December 1924 a hundred children were taken to the Playhouse to see a performance of "Scrooge" by the Pupil Teachers' Centre.

Shortly after taking up his appointment, Trewick admitted two boys - George Nicholson, age 9, from the Roman Catholic school who could not read "even the smallest words" and could do no sums, and Joe W. Staples, age 12, from Australia, who had not been to school, he knew his alphabet but also could not read "even the little words". Staples made rapid improvement, and he was one of the boys in the first photograph of good attenders taken in July 1897 (and it is his copy of the photograph which is reproduced). His younger brother was already in the school according to this message written on the blackboard in July 1916: "Best wishes to British

School children from Corporal Arthur H. Staples of the Australian Engineers, ASF, once a scholar in this school (1892-1900)". Perhaps it was this family who created the school's link with Australia, shown by the consignment of apples which arrived in June 1923. The Australian flag was presented to the school by the Hon. J.M. Whear, Agent General of Victoria, 250 parents and visitors were present and the children put on a programme of physical education, singing and dancing.

Children wore boots to school: in April 1899 Trewick noted that J. and L. Lill had been taken away from school "because the master spoke to them about coming repeatedly with dirty boots". Their father wrote that "if the master wished the boots cleaned he must bring the blacking and do them himself". On the other hand, Jack Drury in the infants was absent for two weeks in November 1908 because of lack of boots. A sign of times to come was in 1912 when Mrs. Earley, the mother of girls in the school, gave a lesson to the upper girls on How to Wash and Dress a Baby. And in 1917 the school had singing practice in the yard for National Baby Week.

The Great War years were a difficult time for the school, particularly when in September 1914 the rooms had to be reorganised to accommodate up to 150 children from Trinity School as theirs was occupied by soldiers. However, the children worked well "in spite of Zeppelin alarms" (German airships, April 1916), and a few days later Empire Day was celebrated singing patriotic songs for Mayor Christopher Adlard. The children also sang at the Town Hall in April 1917 when Gen Von Dorop presented Sergeant C.D. Taylor (an old boy of the school) with the DCM for bravery at Gallipoli, and the Borough presented him with a wristlet watch and a silver cigarette case.

In the difficult months of early 1926, Mr. Beetlestone found that the boys' desks were in a very untidy state: "they contained many scraps of used paper, useless books, copies of Punch, Boys Own paper, worthless novelettes etc." (he soon had them cleaned out). In 1926 the classes were arranged according to children's ability but the inspector's subject reports for 1927 and 1928 were mixed. In needlework the course of work was "too haphazard, both on paper and in practice". A variety of garments were made (and sent to the hospital), "sewing and finishing was fair, but there was excessive use of the sewing machine"(!). Only 18 girls could go each week to the Technical School for housecraft, and with 98 eligible it meant that some did not get any; it was suggested that "this type of work should prove especially useful to a dull and backward group of girls" (a comment which would hardly get by today). Religious Knowledge: "great credit to the headmaster and teachers - every group acquitted themselves creditably. A group of mentally deficient children answered surprisingly well (not the way it would be phrased now). Prayers reverently said, but a supply of new Bibles would help".

In the 1920s children from Eastfield Road, Victoria Road and Keddington Road attended the Trinity School until the age of 11 and then went to Kidgate for the remaining three years. It was the tradition that all boys aged 11 who arrived at Kidgate were dropped over the playground wall into the street.

As a footnote, one is pleased to note that in April 1928 the first class visited the Museum, when C.S. Carter was honorary Curator, and had a lecture on Prehistoric Man. When a class visited in Museums Week 1996, it was a more hands-on experience when they made their own bricks using wooden moulds.

What was this event in the 1920s — a choir?

56

Coughs and
Contagious Diseases

COUGHS and colds were, and still are, regular occurrences in a school, particularly in winter. They seldom rated in mention in the logbooks unless attendances were substantially affected. In January 1866 coughs were prevalent among "the poorer classes especially those residing in the parts adjacent to the river", and in March whooping cough round the Riverhead; in November 1882 and March 1892 many were absent with whooping cough and colds, and in May 1895 ten girls were absent with whooping cough for up to ten weeks. Infants could be particularly badly affected: in March 1900 coughing was so bad that teachers were unable to make themselves heard. There was whooping cough and bronchitis among the infants in November 1903; the Medical Officer of Health closed the department in January 1904 because of whooping cough but when it re-opened in January the coughing of those in school was still "quite distressing", the weather having been cold and raw, and one by, Gordon Brown, did not return until April after an absence of thirteen months. The Infants department was closed for three weeks by the Medical Officer of Health, Dr. W.J. Best, in January 1908, because of whooping cough, and again for a similar period in February 1912. Spanish 'flu struck the school in July 1918, and in mid-November it was closed for a month.

Influenza is usually associated with cold weather, and so it was that in January and February 1922 when severe snow made the streets almost impassable and children from Fotherby could not come by train, the school was closed for a fortnight because of 'flu. The school re-opened on 27thFebruary only to have a holiday on 28th for Princess Mary's wedding. Two years later in February 1924, influenza again caused the school to be closed for two weeks. Attendance in February 1927 fell to 78% because of an influenza epidemic, colds and 'flu reduced attendance to 69% in February 1932, 189 children were absent from the same cause on 19th January 1933 and four days later the morning attendance was only 34%. Influenza struck again in January 1937 and when attendance fell to 55% the Medical Officer of Health closed the school for two weeks.

Scarlatina or scarlet fever was very much a 19th century affliction recorded in the logbooks in 1863 and 1864, 1868 (in November attendance was poor through a combination of scarlet and typhus fever, measles and smallpox), 1877 (George Naylor died in June and other children of the family were excluded from the school for a month), 1890 and 1897. The reference to "the fever" in the girls' logbook for April and May 1889 was probably scarlet fever, affecting first a family of three - Elizabeth, Ellen and Louisa Bell - who were away for three weeks. The mistress, Miss Paull, was so concerned about prolonged illness in the school that she sent all the girls into the playground whenever the weather permitted, and when they had to remain in school musical drill was substituted for normal lessons. Typhoid and typhus fever were only recorded four times: January 1864, November and December 1868, October 1898 (when four children of the Patrick family were affected), and as late as January 1921 (pupil teacher Marjorie Moody).

The town's Medical Officer of Health from the mid-1870s was Dr. Richard Dominichetti, and in July 1881 he gave the following instructions for disinfecting the classrooms: place a piece of sulphur about three inches long on a shovelful of live coals for two hours and then open the windows and doors; this was done on a Saturday. Milk of sulphur had been used in

Class 2

1920s

Class 3

July 1863 to treat ulcerated wounds on boys' legs which had been caused by great heat (it must have been a hot summer). In June 1903 attendance of infants was poor due to nettle rash, while in contrast broken chilblains were noted in February 1907.

The rules laid down for Louth schools by the Medical Officer of Health were quite specific: for scarlet fever no child is to return to school until six weeks at least have elapsed, and then only if there is no peeling of the hands; for measles three weeks is the earliest period after which a child may return and then only if there is no cough; and for whooping cough a child may return if the characteristic whoop has entirely disappeared. And these rules applied to all children of a family affected.

Contagious diseases such as measles (particularly) and mumps occurred a number of times, causing low attendances and sometimes closure: January 1885 with 17 absent and more cases in February; two families in July 1889; March and April 1890 and over a three week period among the infants in March 1892. In October 1893 there were some forty girls affected by measles; in January 1897 the Infants department closed for three weeks and in December 1899 for a month. The whole school closed for four days in July 1905 and for nine weeks in November; when it re-opened in February 1906 the infants mistress complained that "the children have forgotten a great deal". The Infants had to close for two weeks in January 1923, and in February and March 1925 attendances fell as "children kept falling down with mumps and measles". In February the following year the headmaster (William Forster) went to see the Medical officer of Health (Dr. Edward Sharpley) for a ruling on exclusion of measles contacts and was told, "Please yourself - the epidemic is so widespread that it makes no difference". Mumps sometimes occurred with measles but became an epidemic on its own in winter 1938-39 when the Medical Officer of Health closed the school for a week, and in December 1944 mumps was the cause of attendance falling to 67%.

The 1907 Education Act required Lindsey Education Authority to provide medical inspections. A survey the next year of children at elementary schools showed that 18% had tonsilar enlargements and adenoids,, and the Medical Officer commented that "the regular use of the toothbrush is practically unknown". The Infants logbook for 1914 records that the nurse appointed by the County Council examined all the children, and that later in the year there was an inspection by Dr. Perry Walker, one of two Lindsey County Council Medical Officers (he lived at Fernbank on Newmarket). The first logbook record of the School Dentist visiting was in March 1924, followed in September by a talk to the upper Standards on Care of Teeth.

Smallpox is recorded only once (1868) and scabies once (1916), but chickenpox was noted among girls and infants in 1897, 1903, 1906, 1919 (when only 29 of 83 infants were present), 1925, 1933, and 1937. Isolated cases of diphtheria were noted in 1906 and 1916, but in 1939 the school was closed for three weeks by Dr. W.J. Kerrigan because of an epidemic and the whole school was immunised. Cases of ringworm were recorded six times in the period 1902 to 1906, the headmaster (Joseph Trewick) noting that "ringworm has made its appearance and three boys are excluded from school until better". In October 1911 two girls were excluded because of dirty heads, but when they returned they were "still not free from nits".

When the Open Air School for sickly children opened in July 1918, nine children from Kidgate were sent there. It was behind the Technical College in James Street but was badly damaged in the Louth flood of May 1920 and eventually moved to Julian Bower.

The Ropewalk, now part of the playing field.

Proclamation of King Edward VII in the
Market Place, between snow showers, January 1901.

High Days and Holidays

THE SCHOOL YEAR has always been in three terms, but the pattern of holidays has changed. The breaks at Christmas and Easter were a week only, and the four weeks in summer was arranged to fit in with harvesting operation: mid-August to mid-September in 1863 and 1869 but mid-July to mid-August in 1868 for example. If the harvest was unfinished attendance was usually low, and boys could be haymaking in July or gleaning in September, but by the end of the century the dates became more stable at roughly five weeks from late July to early September. However, because of the lateness of the harvest in 1879, the Borough of Louth used powers invested in them by the Education Act of 1876 to "exempt from the prohibitions and restrictions of the Act the employment of children above the age of eight years for the necessary operation of husbandry and the gathering of crops until 11th October".

When the management committee decided in 1872 to have a fortnight holiday at Christmas, the headmaster, Edward Rogers, noted that it was "rather against my inclination which tended towards one week only". Seven years later the committee took a different view and closed for a week at

Christmas and a week at Easter instead of two weeks at Christmas, but by 1890 the fortnight holiday at Christmas was established.

The Bank Holiday Act of 1871 added boxing Day, Easter Monday, Whit Monday and the first Monday in August to the existing statutory holidays of Christmas Day and Good Friday. It took some time for these to get into regular usage, particularly Whit Monday. In 1873 Edward Rogers opened the school on Whit Monday (2nd June) which also by mayoral proclamation had been declared a public holiday, but did not record how many children attended. His successor, James Hargreaves, did close the school on Whit Monday 1880, in line with the resolution of a public meeting in the Town Hall which pledged "to observe the first Monday in June as a general holiday in any year when Whit Monday occurs in May week" (that week being important for the trade of the town). The Wednesday in that week (mid-May) was always a holiday on the occasion of May Day Wednesday or just the May Fair into at least the 1920s.

In the last century there was a half-day holiday in April for the Hiring Statute when farm workers and servants stood in the Market Place and Cornmarket waiting to be hired for the next year by farmers. Other fairs which merited a holiday were at Candlemas (February) and Martinmas (November), and attendance was usually thin on the occasion of big sheep (spring) and cattle fairs (autumn), and there was a day holiday for the Louth Steeplechase (March or April) and the annual ploughing match (November). The school also had special holidays when the Lincolnshire Agricultural Show visited Louth in July in 1878, 1889, 1899, 1909 and 1926, but only a half day in 1936. (The last time the Show visited Louth was in 1949). There was a day or half-day holiday for the annual United Sunday Schools Gala in the summer (although in the 1930s this turned into three half-days over a fortnight as the Sunday Schools held separate galas), and also on the occasion of the Great Temperance Festival (October 1863), Band of Hope Festival (September 1865), and major bazaars in the Town Hall. Attendances were inevitably small when Sanger's Circus (in the area of the present Cattle Market) and Wombwell's or Bostock's Menagerie (in the Market Place) came to the town every year through to the 1920s and usually a half-day holiday was granted.

Royal occasions, national and local events (including funerals) meant that the school was closed for half a day or a day:

March 1864:	Christening of the son of the Prince of Wales.
August 1866:	Laying the foundation stone of the Town Hall.
October 1868:	Funeral of Dr. Samuel Trought (school committee member and former Mayor).
June 1872:	Funeral of J.B. Sharpley (President of the school committee).
June 1887:	Queen Victoria's Golden Jubilee (2 days).
January 1892:	Procession to St. James's church to mark the funeral of HRH the Duke of Clarence.
October 1892:	Funeral of James Fowler, five times Mayor of Louth.
March 1897:	Funeral of Rev. Alben Sayer (United Free Methodist minister).
June 1897:	Queen Victoria's Diamond Jubilee (week).
January 1900:	Relief of Ladysmith (Boer Wars)
May 1900:	Relief of Mafeking (Boer Wars). Children sang patriotic songs 9-10 a.m. Met 6 p.m. and marched to Market Place where several songs were sung accompanied by band. Each child presented with a cake and an orange.
January 1901:	Proclamation of King Edward VII in the Market Place (snowing heavily).
June 1902:	Peace in South Africa.
June 1902:	Coronation of Edward VII (4 days).
July 1903:	Funeral of Ald. Barnard Longbottom (school manager).
September 1905:	To see General Booth (Salvation Army) pass through the town in his motor car.
December 1910:	Declaration of Poll, General Election.

June 1911:	Coronation of King George V (week).
June 1912:	To see B.C. Hucks and his flying machine.
October 1917:	To see General Sir J. Maxwell present a Military Medal in the Market Place. (Was it to former pupil Joseph Plant?).
November 1918:	Armistice.
July 1919:	Peace Celebrations (2 days).
June 1920:	Funeral of Louth Flood victims and General Election (2 days).
April 1923:	Duke of York's wedding.
May 1924:	Educational Exhibition in the Town Hall (3 afternoons).
May 1935:	King George V and Queen Mary Silver Jubilee.
January 1936:	Funeral of King George V.
May 1937:	Coronation of King George VI.
July 1944:	Local Prisoner of War event.
May 1945:	VE Celebrations (2 days).
July 1945:	General Election.
March 1947:	Closed 2 weeks (3rd-14th) because of lack of fuel.

On the occasion of the proclamation of Edward VIII on Wednesday 22nd January 1936, the children listened on the radio to the broadcast from St. James's Palace, and at noon went to hear the Mayor of Louth read the proclamation. Other occasions when the children went out of school included going to see the Panorama of Africa in the Town Hall (December 1870), 10th Lincolnshire Regiment marching through the town (September 1897), visit to the Japan-Britain Exhibition at the White City (July 1910), visit to the Festival of Empire Exhibition at the Crystal Palace (July 1911), a matinee at the Picture Palace (now Wilkinson's) in aid of the Serbians (December 1915), and a visit to the Wembley Exhibition (June 1924); 54 children taken and those aged over eleven were each given 3s - the day after).

In June 1868 the North Lincolnshire Rifles were in camp at Thornton Abbey and on Wednesday 24th headmaster David

*The arch built over Ramsgate for the Lincolnshire
Agricultural Show at Louth in 1909.*

*Louth Volunteers march down Eastgate on the occasion
of the Coronation of King George V, June 1911.*

CATALOGUE OF
Bostock & Wombwell's
Royal Menagerie

(Established by the late George Wombwell in 1805.)

Visitors will please note that, as the management are continually supplying and exchanging specimens with Zoological Gardens, the following exhibits and their catalogued numbers are subject to occasional variations.

The Leucoryx Antelope.

The Tapir, or River Elephant.

10. Emeu, or Australian Ostrich.

The largest of all birds (with one exception, the African ostrich). The emeu has neither tongue, wing, nor tail, and every quill on its body bears two distinct feathers. In Australia the emeu is coursed in the same manner as the hare is coursed in this country, and it must be a very swift horse or dog that can overtake them.

20. Nosegus, or Slenderbeak Cockatoos, from Australia.

30. Blue and Scarlet Macaws.

40. Blue and Orange Macaws, from the Brazils.

The largest and most beautiful of the parrot family.

50. European Storks, from Denmark.

60. The Griffin Vulture, from the Himalayas.

Great discussion has at various times been maintained among naturalists as to whether the well-known faculty of vultures, by which they discover a dying carcase from distances which appear almost in-

McMichael noted that "this is review day, many of the boys' fathers and other relatives are letting off a little of their intense military spirit today, ergo many little boys who ought to be in school are at home minding shop or house for father or mother who are at Thornton". One half-day holiday which became an institution started with the opening of the Louth to Mablethorpe railway on Wednesday 17th October 1877; the following day there were cheap excursions (only 6d return in 1889), and thereafter the nearest date became known as Mablethorpe Thursday with special half-day excursions and continued until just after the turn of the century.

Springside Steps — one of the ways to and from school.

Back (L-R): *R Addison, G Lambert, S Powell, B Hewson, Joe Atkinson, Brian Street, Cyril Graves, F Riggall.* 3rd row: *George Cash, Harry Simpson, Cyril Spencer, John Taylor, Lambert, Cyril Laughton, Arthur Connors, Ray Coulsey, Les Ferriby, W Pridmore, Bill Arnold.* 2nd row: *George King, Len Jaines, Cyril Larder, John Briggs, Doug Norton, —, Papworth, —, S Bradley, George Grebby, Les Hunter.* Front: *Dennis Goodwin, Jim Dalton, Eric Dexter, Dick Walsh, D Wrisdale, Farrow, Newsome*

1932

Names not known

The New Era

WHEN the school reopened after extensive remodelling on 9th September 1930 as Kidgate County Junior Mixed, the new headmaster, Percy Latter, had a staff of nine women teachers and a roll of 456 children. The teachers and classes were:

Miss E.A. Bontoft - 53 babies, mixed; Miss M.M. Woodward (she died in 1933 and was replaced by Miss C.J. Milburn who left to marry in 1940) - 47 infants, mixed; and Mrs. G. Broddle - 60, transition class; these were in three classrooms in the 1850 extension;

Miss E. Giddings (she died in 1940) - 47 girls; Miss M.H. Hibbitt - 50 girls; and Miss Bridgewater (she left to marry in 1937 and was replaced by Arthur Southwell) - 45 girls; these were in three classrooms in the original girls' room;

Miss H.M. Johnson (later Mrs. Murfitt, 1932, resigned 1937 and succeeded by Miss N. Drury) - 51 boys; Miss E. Kent - 53 boys; and Mrs. Mason (she retired in 1950) - 50 boys: in three classrooms in the original boys' room.

Only three of the teachers were certificated - Mrs. Broddle, Miss Giddings and Miss Bridgewater. Later in the term the classes became mixed according to the children's attainments.

Present at the reopening were the Chairman, Mr. B.C. Hall, and Vice-Chairman, Mr. J.R. Coney, of the Managers of the Louth Council Schools (including Eastfield Road and Monks' Dyke). The Director of Education for Lindsey, Mr. S. Maudson Grant, and LEA Inspector Mr. J.W. Twidale visited the school, and parents were able to look over the buildings. The first term in the new school included a double session to allow children to leave early for the circus in October, the observance of Armistice Day including an address to the top classes on the League of nations, an open day for parents in December which became a regular event with up to 300 parents visiting, and a Christmas party with tea, concert and a visit from Santa Claus on the last day of term.

The following February the out-of-date long desks were replaced with desks from the Newmarket (Wesleyan) school, and in April children from Fotherby were transferred to Eastfield Road. In May, Mary Simpson won the main prize in the national Ovaltine essay competition (of 14,800 competitors) and eight other children in the school also won prizes. (In 1936 thirty-nine children won a box of chocolates in the Bournvita essay competition). There were the usual half days for the Sunday School galas, but "inclement weather spoilt the sports afternoon" in July.

The first Board of Education report noted "the pleasant and convenient accommodation" while regretting the absence of a hall. Sections of that report are worth quoting in full:

"Transfers to the new Senior School (Monks' Dyke Council) are made at the end of each term following the pupils' eleventh birthday, for reasons which do not seem to outweigh the disadvantages which follow so frequent an upheaval in every class. Moreover the system of terminal promotions works to the disadvantage of some children who are compelled to take the annual school examination for scholarships shortly after the inevitable unsettlement arising from this transfer to fresh teachers and the new environment of the Senior School.

The school has made a very satisfactory beginning. An

excellent tone and a good working spirit pervades all the classes. The children are plainly happy in their various activities, in which they find much that holds their interest. In the last year of their stay, the boys and girls are separated in two classes for the subjects of fundamental importance. These children are keen and have developed a self-confidence which displays itself in a very willing and intelligent response. In the boys class the teaching of Arithmetic is very successful, while the girls can be equally commended for the excellence of their spoken and written English. The combined singing of these two classes is also noticeably good.

Although there are classes of slower children where less ground is covered there are no markedly weak spots in the school, having regard to the material of which these classes are constructed. There appears to be some distrust of the powers of the younger children to launch out on "free" writing as distinct from the composition of simple isolated sentences. Moreover the children might be provided with a better supply of suitable stories in their conversation lessons.

While some matters of detail are included in the introductions to History which would be better left to the Senior School, there are wider aspects of the story of mankind which, with advantage, could be more fully utilised in the higher classes of the department."

The report on the Scripture examination in November 1932 was even more complimentary. "A most happy tone pervades this school. This was the first examination in Religious Knowledge since being re-organised as a Junior and Infants Department, and we could not fail to be impressed by the earnest aim of the headmaster, most keenly supported by his conscientious staff, to make the religious instruction of lasting value in the lives of those under his care. The written exercises showed a thorough knowledge of the Bible stories with a real application to daily life. This was also noticeable in the oral work. The singing of the hymns really meant something to those little ones and was especially good in the Senior class."

When two Managers, Rev. W.A. Hind and Bert Appleby, visited the school in February 1933 they were "delighted with the tone and discipline. The humorous happiness and good manners of the children were most noticeable", and when other managers visited in September, they said that "the whole tone and spirit of the school makes every visit a pleasure". And there was a letter from the LEA in December 1936 congratulating the headmaster and staff on receiving such an excellent report on the school. Was this the reason why the LEA and the Inspector gave permission for the senior children to go to the Playhouse to see the film "David Copperfield"?

Empire Day 1933 (24th May) was marked by "appropriate lessons", an address by the headmaster to senior children, a visit from the Mayor, Cllr. Jesse Rushforth, who addressed the whole school in the playground and the National Anthem was sung. When Miss Kent was ill that year the supply teacher brought in was Miss Mabel Hare of Horncastle (I remember her a few years later as a strict teacher at the Queen Elizabeth's Grammar School, Horncastle). Miss Joyce Towle was another supply teacher. And in October Alderman William Lacey donated a Whirligig to the school; was this a spinning toy or a small roundabout? (rather than the other definition - an instrument for punishing petty offenders!)

In-service teacher training was still part of school life but in a different form. The school was closed for a day in July 1934 as most of the teachers were attending a refresher course in Lincoln about the new Board of Education Physical Education syllabus, and the following February the headmaster met with other junior school heads on four occasions after school about arithmetic teaching. There were courses at Derby attended by Miss Kent (1936) and Miss Bontoft (1937), on infants teaching at Lincoln (Miss Giddings 1939), and in 1936 Miss Milburn attended a National Savings conference at Buxton.

Students from Lincoln and other Training Colleges came to the school for teaching observation and practice. These included Miss Joyce Smith (Furzedown) in 1936; she joined the

1935

Back (L-R): *Joan Ferrey, Rita Jackson, Barbara Crosby, Olive Gee, Mary Wherry, Marjorie Sharpe, Sybil Cresswell, Betty Sutton, Lucy Johnson, Viola Taylor, Joan Hyde, Chris Cersey.* Centre: *Sheila Plumpton, Beryl Paul, Bella Hunter, Cecily Sharp, Edna Mee, Pam Hall, Joan England, Gilliam Clark, Mary Smithson, Freda Livsey, Kath Cribb, Rita Matthews, Kath Hall, Alma Lacey.* Front: *Nancy Eversham, Margaret Goy, Audrey Good, Madge Stebbings, Gwen Ganney, Mabel Forman, Winney Fell, Gwen Dring, Myra Goddard, Gwen Parrish, Marian Jackson, Cecily Drewery.*

Bateson's Swimming Bath

75

staff in November 1940 and the same month married Jack Prowting. Also Miss Millie Ingram (Lincoln), Miss K. Goodwin, Miss Joyce Towle and Miss Maisie Osbourne (1935), Miss Kathleen Marshall (Homerton) and Mr. M. Hibbitt in 1937 and Miss Marie Towle (Lincoln) in 1938. When Mrs. Prowting left in 1943 she was replaced by Mrs. M. Butterwick. Miss I. Giddings also joined the staff in November 1940 and married Mr. C.B. Dawson in April 1944. During the difficult war years there were a number of supply teachers including Mrs. D. Codd, Miss Helen Moore, and Miss Gwen Leake who had won a scholarship from the school in 1933.

The virtues of drinking milk were being propagated and Miss Pembroke of the Milk Publicity Council visited the school to give talks to the children; and in January 1936 the logbook records that four children were allowed free milk by the LEA. Swimming instruction in the summer months started in 1937 at the baths in Maiden Row (now Church street), for classes 1A, 1B, 2A and 2B, with swimming sports in July.

Out of school activities included a visit by classes 1A, 1B and 2A to the pea factory on Newbridge Hill to see the process of canning, the Louth Schools Music Festival in 1936 and 1937 when the school closed for the day (the school won the Hospital Cup in 1937), and school trips to London (1936), Oxford (1938) and Liverpool (1939). In May 1938 several children from Manby applied for admission, but this was refused as they would have taken the number on the roll above the maximum of 400. An unpleasant incident happened in June 1937 when the school was broken into and drawers and desks were forced in the headmaster's room and five classrooms.

In the summer before the outbreak of the Second World War there were first aid lectures for teachers and a visit about air raid precautions. The effects of war were felt immediately the school re-opened in September, as 30 evacuees and two teachers from Leeds had to be absorbed into the school. A double shift system was instituted: Classes 1A, 1B, 2A and 3A - 9 am to 12.30 pm and Classes 2B, 3B and Infants 1-3 - 1.30 pm to 4 pm. Was it just coincidence that within three weeks there was a diphtheria epidemic and the school had to be closed for three weeks? However, the evacuees were transferred to St. Michael's school in November and the school returned to a normal timetable and the winter hours of 9 am to 11.45 am and 1 pm to 3.15 pm. During the snowy winter of January-February 1940 the boiler burst and the school had to be closed for ten days until repairs were effected. By the end of February the school reverted to "summer" times of 9 am to 12 noon and 1.15 pm to 3.45 pm.

In March 1940 a former pupil, Leslie Bradley who had served on HMS Ajax visited the school; another, private W. Marshall who had spent seventeen years in Edmonton, Canada also visited and spoke to the children. There was a gasmask inspection, windows were papered against bomb shattering, war gardening commenced in April, there were air raids in June (one reduced attendance to 44%) and assemblies were held at 10 am, reverting to 9 am in September. There were more air raid warnings in January, February and March 1941, but the air raid shelters were not completed until September. Teacher Arthur Southwell and the school caretaker, Mr. Bell, were called up in September 1940. The new caretaker was Mr. G.R. Winteringham until Mr. Bell returned in June 1946, but he left the next year and was replaced by Mr. Bruce. Mr. Southwell returned in October 1945.

Collecting paper salvage was part of the school's war effort and it won the monthly Salvage Shield in November 1942. War savings totalled £1,339 13s 9d for the year ending September 1942, and in Salute the Soldier Week in June 1944, £2,068 6s 7d was raised. The summer holiday in 1943 was re-arranged into two parts - 6th-30th August and 17th September to 18th October. The annual Christmas party continued to be held, and in 1943 it was "a very happy time". There were again difficulties with the heating system in October 1944, and the school had to be closed for a week.

When news of Germany's unconditional surrender was received on Monday 7th May 1945, a short service of thanksgiving and prayer was held in all classrooms at 3.30 pm. The Mayor's Victory Treat for the children was in October with a concert in the Playhouse and tea in the Town Hall. Empire

Day in May was marked with a "wireless ceremony for schools". The school closed for polling on the day of the General Election, 5th July.

Two students on teaching observation that year were Miss M. Espin (Lincoln Training College) and Brian Howe before he went up to Caius College, Cambridge, with Miss Jean Darnell in January 1946. A visitor in 1945 had been the former PT Organiser, Miss Terry (she was the one who twenty-five years before had been pleased with "the deep breathing"). Rationing was still with us in 1946, so a gift of sweets from Argentina, organised by the WVS, was very welcome.

Student Miss Sheila Martin (she won a scholarship from the school in 1940, later became Mrs. Greenfield and went on to become a headmistress) just completed her teaching practice in January 1947 before prolonged snow and frost disrupted the school with closure for two weeks in early March due to lack of fuel. By June however there was again swimming at the Baths. In July Mr. H. Willerton from Cleethorpes joined the staff, initially for one term, but in fact he stayed until 1958 when he moved to the Secondary Modern School in Skegness. At the end of the summer term 1947 there was a concert, tea party and presentation to Mr. Latter on his retirement. He wrote in the logbook: "This being the last school day of my career I say farewell with feelings of regret for the severance to myself, but with all good wishes for the future success of the school". He had certainly served well over the first seventeen years of the new era to give a firm foundation for the future, and he paid a return visit ten years later.

The new headmaster was Frank Lamming, and it was in his time that the school assumed its present name of Kidgate County Primary. During the next two years Miss Sylvia Wilson (a former scholarship-winning pupil who later became Deputy Head at the school) and Miss Jean Pinder did a period of teaching practice, Cyril Jackson joined the staff from Lancaster Emergency Training College, and Mrs. M.E. O'Houlihan worked as a temporary assistant until she went to Emergency Training College (the emergency being the need to train more teachers quickly after wartime losses). Of the 72 children who left in

1948, 15 went to the Grammar Schools and 53 to Monks' Dyke. In April 1949 there were 394 children on the roll; in September 1952 the roll was 384 with 83 children competing for the remaining 16 places. Corporal punishment was still being used: two boys received "a stroke of the cane" for playing truant, and another went to court for stealing (October 1950). In December 1951 the Mayor, Cllr. A.W. Jaines (father of the Mayor in 1996-97 Mrs. Margaret Ottaway) entertained all the pupils to tea and a concert of carols in the Town Hall.

According to the Louth Advertiser, Mr. Lamming "enthused such scholastic ardour into his charges that many of them are all too anxious not to leave school at the end of normal hours but to stay on and continue with their work". One such occasion was a visit by 80 of the older children to the agricultural engineers W.E. Harness Ltd., linked to a BBC school radio broadcast, to look at some of the machinery "mentioned over the air". A number of pupils became so interested that they "spent several hours on cycles chasing up firms and farmers gleaning all they can about the industry". Mr. Lamming was quoted as saying "We should use the amenities of our own neighbourhood, and let the children learn about them, as well as labouring over the old inevitable sums about taps filling baths with water at such-and-such a rate".

From further afield he received three letters in June 1952. One was from a former assistant teacher, John Waite, who had been known in Louth as a motorcycle racing enthusiast; he was principal of Windfield School at Mackay, Alberta in the Canadian prairies where he had emigrated the previous year, and the children - all ten of them! - also wrote. The third letter was from a former pupil, Valentine Cook, then at school in Toronto, in contrast a school of 56 classrooms and 2,296 pupils.

It was also in 1952 when the "teachers strongly disagreed to having to supervise meals because the dinner supervisors (Mrs. R.L. Hunt and Mrs. B. Pridgeon) had done the job very well for the last five or six years". February 1953 saw some disruption to the normal routine of the school when a total of 26 evacuees and a teacher were admitted from Mablethorpe

Kidgate
County Primary School
LOUTH

THE "CAMM PRIZE"

AWARDED TO

Anne Appleby

FOR

Highest Marks in the "Scholarship" Examination

~~Class Teacher.~~

F. Lamming.
Headmaster.

Date 15 July 1948.

*Anne Appleby received her prize
from Mr Camm in the Town Hall.*

Mrs Mason's top class 1947-48.

because of the disastrous East Coast Flood. Later that year the school won a shield for the highest percentage of savers in Louth schools for the third successive year.

Teachers on the staff during the 1950s were: Mrs. M.H. Hibbitt (she retired in August 1952, having served since the school reopened in 1930, "her kind but firm discipline appreciated"); Miss E. Kent (she retired in April 1960 after 30 years); Mrs. G. Broddle (she retired in December 1960 after 30 years); Mrs. M. Butterick (she had started in 1943 and retired in December 1960); Miss Edith Bontoft (she was due to retire in December 1963, having been connected with the school as pupil and teacher for over forty years, but stayed on for one more term - to May 1964 - because of staff problems); Miss N. Drury; Mrs. L. Freshney (from 1954); Mrs. D.J. Elvin (from 1959); Mr. C. Jackson; Mr. D.E. Williamson (to 1952); Mrs. D.B. Bradshaw (1952-58); Mrs. G.R. Oxby (from 1956); Mr. H. Willerton (to 1958); Mr. D.J. Kempson (to 1958); together with Miss J.F.E. Willetts (later Mrs. Pridgeon), Miss E. Steel and Miss M.J. Dalgleish.

In the 1960s, Mr. Waite taught for one year (1961), and Mrs. B.M. Major and Mrs. W.H. Burgess joined the staff in 1962. Miss Margaret Taylor was Deputy Head for three years (January 1961 to December 1963) and was succeeded in April 1964 by Miss Joan Hewson, and Miss Rowson joined the staff in 1967.

After eight years as headmaster, Frank Lamming left and was succeeded in May 1955 by Clifford Spray; he became the second longest serving head (23 years) by the time he retired in 1978. He saw the formation of the Parent Teacher Association in 1960, and was involved with other headteachers in the town in formulating the "Louth Plan" which was approved by Lindsey County Council and the Secretary of State in 1963. The effect of this was to delay "selection" for the grammar school, which became co-educational, with all Kidgate leavers going to Monks' Dyke High School.

The logbook for this period notes just two unsavoury incidents: September 1962 - "Break-in over weekend by three

children age 7, 6 and 5. The two oldest given a "spanking"";
and January 1964 - "Two ex-pupils, who left last July, broke into
the school".

When Mr Spray took up his appointment, Cinder Lane
was unadopted and there was a house on the corner of Cinder
Lane and Kidgate with a garden along the lane; this was
demolished and the site incorporated into the playground.
That had a wall down the middle which he had removed, and
the toilets were still all outside. There was very little playing
field but over the years land was acquired to extend it to the
present area.

All the desks were old-fashioned cast iron and oak two-
seaters; these were soon replaced by lockers, much more
modern and flexible. The old desks were sold off at 2s 6d each,
and the school did a roaring trade. The school was badly lit,
he recalls, each room having only two 60-watt bulbs. The
Education Authority agreed to do something about it, and four
100-watt bulbs were put in; later fluorescent lights were
installed. The colour scheme in the school was institutional
brown and cream; he asked for colours and the school was
transformed, although the school had to raise £40 towards the
cost.

School meals were eaten in two sittings in the Monks'
Dyke School canteen, which entailed a lot of to-ing and fro-ing
in all weathers. Later an extension was built at the west end of
the school and meals were brought from the kitchens at
Eastfield Road School. They were eaten, again in two sittings,
in two adjoining classrooms, separated by a moveable partition.
The washing-up had to be done in the extension, which wasn't
pleasant for the adjoining class.

A new classroom and corridor with toilets was built at the
east end of the school, and later an assembly hall with kitchen
and indoor toilets for all were built. When building work
began the remains were found of the five air raid shelters which
had only been part demolished. As the numbers on roll began
to increase, four Spooner mobile classrooms were installed next
to the hall, and later the kitchens were removed.

"I enjoyed my time at Kidgate", wrote Mr. Spray. "I considered myself fortunate to have been appointed to such a pleasant school in such a lovely town. The children, with few exceptions, were well behaved and charming."

When Clifford Spray retired in 1978, he was succeeded by Mr. T.H. Thompson,, always just known as "H", and he continued to build on the school's excellent reputation. He moved to Devon as a primary schools inspector in 1991 just before the big 150th celebrations and was presented with a CD player. In turn he gave the school a bird house for the wildlife garden being constructed in the grounds, along with a pair of binoculars and a bird identification book. The present headmaster is Mr. Stuart M. Sizer.

Richard Goulding who won the only Grammar School scholarship in 1880, and went on to be Private Secretary and Librarian to the Duke of Portland.

84

Scholarships

THE first year Louth Grammar School offered free scholarships, in 1879, there were eight, open to Kidgate, St. James, Holy Trinity, Wesleyan, St. Michael and St. Mary. Five boys from Kidgate competed - Ernest Coppin, Fred Hickling, Herbert Brader, Tom Dickinson and John Bradley; the logbook notes that four were successful (together with three from St. James and one from Holy Trinity), but it also records that Coppin and Hickling were paid monitors and then pupil teachers in succeeding years.

In 1880 there was only one vacant scholarship and competition was fierce - fifteen boys including six from Kidgate: it was awarded to Richard W. Goulding, of whom the Grammar School headmaster wrote "He is a good boy and most satisfactory in all his work". Kidgate was the most successful school in gaining scholarships: Alfred Dickinson and John Coppin in 1881 and Alfred Emerson in 1882, making eight in the first four years, compared with St. James four, Wesleyan three, Holy Trinity one and St. Michael one. The next scholarships were in 1895 - Joseph Plant (who won the Military Medal in the Great War) and Charles Donner (he returned as a pupil teacher in 1899).

In a letter to the elementary schools in 1899 the Grammar School headmaster, Canon Hopwood, set out the conditions of the scholarships: Boys must have been educated for three years at a school in Louth and be under the age of 15.

The examination would be in Arithmetic (including decimals) 200 marks, English Grammar (with parsing and analysis) 100, History of England 50, Geography of Great Britain and Ireland 50, Reading 50, Writing 50.

The Lindsey County Council Education Committee having been established in 1893, annual scholarships were offered: two senior at £50 a year, six "A" at £12 and eight "B" at £6. The first from Kidgate was John Todds in 1896, for three years at the Grimsby Higher Grade School. Succeeding awards were to Walter Birkett and Maud Taylor (1900), Frank French, John Wright and John Waters, "A" scholarships for three years (1901), George Camm and Matthew Faulds to the Grimsby Higher Grade School (1902), Frederick Birkett, who also won the Wells Prize of half a guinea (1903), and Sydney Shaw (1911).

The following scholarships to the Grammar School(s) were won by Kidgate pupils up to reorganisation in 1929:

1900 Roy Brocklebank (first on the list)
1901 Horace Sanderson (first on the list)
1903 Alan Wright and Jesse Broughton
1905 Lawrence Lill
1907 Reg Perfect
1908 Walter Lowry (first of 22 candidates)
1909 Rowland Norwood (he also shared the Wells Prize with Oliver Goy)
Winnie Wright and Kathie Sanderson - the first to the Girls' Grammar School which was established in 1903
1911 Nellie Kemp
1913 Evelyn Higginson, Willie Sharp, Edna Lill and Kathie Stamper
1914 Rupert Hill (first on the list), Herbert Bond, Mollie Brocklebank, Mary Skinn and Jessie Browning
1915 William Frost, Eric Farmery, Edith Humphreys and Phyllis Stamper
1916 Eric Teesdale and Joyce Teesdale
1918 Ella Humphreys, Ivy Lombard and Mary Langley

86

1919 Arthur Lowry, Chris Cribb, Robert Fell, Les Shaw, Doris Bontoft, Muriel Farmery, Olive Jacklin and Phyllis Moody

1920 Henry Fell, Willie Platt, Donald Burns, Clifford Mitchell, Norman Fridlington (he was presented with a knife and cricket set for 100% attendance since joining the school), Ivy Platt, Elsie Janney and - Jacklin (her Christian name was not recorded)

Vernon Archer - Fotherby Trust Scholarship

1921 Charles Smith, Eric Lister and John Cribb

1923 Reg Starsmore, Graham Ingleton and Joyce Catchpole

1926 Eric Coulsey, John Maltby, Harold Moncaster, Eliza Norton, Jean Luck, Joan Robertson and Kathleen Dales

1928 John Ranshaw, Hilda Carter and Iris Meanwell

Other scholarships:

1940 Eric Tucker, Royal Naval College, Greenwich

1942 Glyn Price, London County Council

The Lindsey County Council scholarship examinations were taken in two parts, the first in English and Arithmetic at Kidgate and the second in the Boys' and Girls' Grammar Schools. From 1931 to 1946 the names of those obtaining scholarships were proudly displayed on the Honours Boards.

1931	Charles Plumpton	William Eastwood	Frank Shearsmith
	John Maltby	John Bennett	George Bradley
	Muriel Skipworth	Margaret Lane	Doris Lill
	Freda Sandall		
1932	Gwen Boswell	George Cash	Arthur Connors
	Eric Dexter	Harold Newsome	Betty Pedley
	Wilfred Pridmore	Henry Simpson	Richard Walsh
	Joan Wilson		
1933	Gwen Leake	Joan Matthews	Violet Taylor
	Ruby Hullett	Mary Kingswood	Kenneth Arnold
	Harold Jackson	Edward Blackburn	Henry Ward
	Dennis Goodwin	Leslie Ferriby	Alfred Dalton
1934	Geoffrey Howe	Charles Briggs	Lionel Gowing
	Walter Walsh	Jean Ovenden	Nancy Timms
1935	Kathleen Cross	Vera Standley	Nellie Archer
	Vera Lammiman	Ralph Sharp	Edward Jacklin
	Norman Brocklebank	Peter Goodwin	

1936	Geoffrey Wright	Christopher Day	John Smalley
	Peter Pridmore	Tom Briggs	Kenneth Croskell
	Georgina Plumpton	Marjorie Barton	Dorothy Wilson
	Enid Timms	Connie Willey (Anne Pahud Scholarship)	
1937	Alec Dannatt	Rowland Sargent	Cecily Clarke
	Audrey Good	Theresa Littler	Nancy Coote
	Pamela Hall		
1938	Brian Howe	William Rippon	Kenneth Barnes
	Denys Masterman	Ronald Standley	Joyce Brown
	Marjorie Rayner	Margaret Boswell	Jean Darnall
	Phyllis Pridgeon	Kathleen Sylvester	
1939	Barbara Panton	Patricia Warden	Sheila Parrish
	Kathleen Laughton	Monica Cribb	Raymond Skipworth
	Peter Smith	Raymond Hildred	John Topley
	Thomas Clarke	Edward Stringer	
1940	Donald Winter	Sonia Carson	Vera Davis
	Betty Drury	Pauline Espin	Gwendoline Leake
	Sheila Martin	Joan Poore	Sylvia Wilson
	Rita Addison (Anne Pahud Scholarship)		
1941	Ronald Oldham	Clive Ottley	Anthony Teesdale
	Brian Wileman	Jean Atkinson	Joan Bonner
	Joyce Epton	Vera Jesney	Eileen Needham
	Eileen Parrish	Margaret Moncaster (Anne Pahud Scholarship)	
1942	Peter Fridlington	John Maltby	Glyn Price
	Mary Bemrose	Jean Snowden	Gloria Ford
	Gwen Ruffell-Ward	Margaret Darnell	Monica Jackson
1943	Denis Cross	Peter Drury	Gordon Williams
	Standley Nicholson	Gwendoline Walters	Sheila Davey
	Pamela Davis	Margaret Snowden	Jill Lee
1944	Derrick Day	John Rowson	Joan Auested
	Ruth Griffiths (Anne Pahud Scholarship)		
1945	Gordon Croft	Pat Goodwin	Byron Lacey
	Adrian Marshall	Kenneth Oldham	Philip Roberts
	Colin Walter	John Johnson	Christine Botting
	Marlene Blackbourne	Janet Dawson	Pauline Lawrence
	Mary Lee	Florence Perry	Beryl Snowden
	Margaret Wood		
1946	Robert Taylor	David Montgomery	Graham Day
	Derek Peake	Robert Ellis	Gordon Goodall
	Clive Bunn	Alan Dee	Leslie Milson
	Derek Thompson	Trevor Johnson	Diane Milner
	Ann Welch	Margaret Spencer	Betty Pinder
	Monica Davey	Betty Hammond	Freda Fytche
	Maureen Dickinson		

From 1947 there are unfortunately no Christian names on the lists recorded, and those for 1949 and 1950 are referred to as admissions to the Grammar Schools from Kidgate, and thereafter only numbers with percentage of the age group; for four years no names are recorded in the logbook. After 1964 the Louth Plan came into operation.

1947   Boys: W.A. Davey, T. Drew, B. Damms, G. Gibson, P. Killick, D. Miles, M. Moore, M. Short, G. Stephenson, B. Stephenson, D. Vinter, S. Waite, P. Roberts.

         Girls: H. Darnell, S. Eyre, G. Martin, S. Martin, M. Reed, M. Stephenson, P. Wood.

1948   Boys: R.J. Goodall, E.B. Graves, D. Hewson, J. Kirk, M.A. Lee, D.B. Milson, K.C. Robinson.

         Girls: A. Appleby, M. Barker, C.G. Brown, J.C. Fairey, J. Johnson, H.A. Mack, D.M. Moncaster, S.K. Taylor.

This was the first year of the Camm Prize awarded for the highest marks in the scholarship examination, and won by Anne Appleby.

1949   Boys: B.J. Annal, R. Brumby, R.B. Chatterton, G. Dobb, M. Eyre, V.D. Fairey, P.A. Fenton, D.E. Gibson, M.D. Gillender, K.E. Janney, A.K. Jesney, R.J. Killick, K.B. Needham, J.L. Parker, G.A. Pollard, D. Taylor, B. Turner, H.J. Walters, B.R. Ward.

         Girls: V.C. Birmingham, D.M. Miller, D.J. Moncaster M.E. Montgomery, J. Murfitt, R.J. Taylor.

1950   Boys: D.E. Beard, J.R.C. Glover, J.E. Hoare, J.G. Lee, J. Metcalfe, N.A. Pottergill, J.W. Wiggen.

         Girls: M. Cheeseman, C.L. Horner, J. Horstead, J.R. Mawer, N.A. Naulls, E.J. Snowden.

1954   6 boys and 13 girls (above the county average)
1957   11 boys and 8 girls
1958   8 boys and 15 girls (35.4%)
1959   6 boys and 2 girls (19.5%)
1960   10 boys and 6 girls (35%)
1961   9 boys and 11 girls (38.5%)
1962   12 boys and 6 girls (37.5%)
1963   6 boys and 17 girls (50%)
1964   7 boys and 10 girls (33%)

A Weather Report

INCLEMENT WEATHER (usually rain and snow) has always affected attendances and in some cases early closure of the school, but the logbooks are also a useful source of weather records.

1863 September 22:	Heavy rains, many children late.
1864 February 5:	Snow - many absent.
February 22:	Snow - allowed children to attend panorama.
August 9:	Very wet - no country children.
1865 January 26:	Snowing and thawing - dangerous walking.
November 23:	Very heavy gale.
1866 February 28:	Deep snow and severe NE wind.
June 4:	Great storm at noon.
November 16:	Great rains - many roads and streets impassable.
1867 January 14-18:	Deep snow, small attendance.
1868 June 19:	Continues unusually fine and dry.
July 16:	Awful hot and dry - children do very little work.
1870 February 7:	Very wet, only 96 boys present.
July 8:	Intensely hot, children unwell in school.
December 7,12,27:	Heavy snow.
1871 January 2:	Weather extremely severe.
January 4:	Frost has lasted a fortnight.

1871	January 11:	Snow again.
	February 10:	Heavy snowfall, worst during a very severe winter.
1874	March 7:	Heavy snow, only 6 girls present.
	September 24:	Severe thunderstorm with lightning 2 pm.
	November 30:	Bitterly cold this week.
	December 7:	Weather severe.
1876	February 14:	Heavy snow.
1881	January 21:	Great snowstorm.
1888	January 30:	Very stormy morning.
	March 14:	Snow, only 31 infants present.
1889	November 27:	Severe snowstorm, 29 girls only, sent home.
	November 28:	Girls from the country unable to get in because of the state of the roads.
1890	March 20:	Very wet morning, only 70 girls in.
	November 27:	Severe snowstorm.
1891	January 15:	Severe snowstorm.
	January 23:	Severe weather, attendance 10% down.
1892	January 11:	Severe weather, poor attendance.
	March 10:	Very poor attendance; many had got feet and clothes wet; weather continued bad; holiday in afternoon "owing to stress of weather".
	September 21:	Exceedingly rough and wet, only 54 boys at 9.30 am; waited until somewhat abated and children dismissed at 10.30 am; holiday given for afternoon.
	December 8:	Severe weather caused many children to be kept at home.
1895	January 28:	Heavy fall of snow, only 89 boys, 60 girls and 31 infants.
	January 30:	Severe snowstorm.
	October 16:	Very bad morning, only 29 infants.
	October 20:	Weather very bad.

1899 March 20:	Very cold and snowy morning.
March 23:	Snow very deep, only 35 infants.
1900 June 20:	Heavy thunderstorm 1.20 pm, many children drenched; when storm had cleared whole school sent home.
1902 March 21:	As school assembled in afternoon large number of children caught in sudden heavy shower of rain; all sent home.
1904 November 22:	Very severe snowstorm.
November 26:	Continuing bad weather.
1905 January 16:	Cold and windy; temperature in Room 1 never above 36 F; in other rooms highest was 46 F.
1906 February 9:	Temperature in school below 40 F.
1907 January 25:	Weather very severe. Ink frozen in the wells at 10 am.
1916 March 3:	Snow and sleet make roads very bad.
March 28:	Terrible snowstorm.
1920 May 29:	School gardens "utterly destroyed" in heavy rain (which caused Louth Flood).
1931 January 30:	Very bad snowstorm.
March 10:	Heavy snowfall, large numbers absent.
1932 February 10:	(Ash Wednesday): Snowfall, attendance 69%.
1935 January 28:	Snow, low attendance.
1940 January 22-24:	Very heavy snowfall, attendances 56%, 68% and 72%.
January 31- February 1:	More snow; attendances 59%, 57%.
July 26:	School struck by lightning 4 pm.
1947 January 27:	Snow.
February 4-11:	Bad snowy weather; Mrs. Mason (Class 1 Boys) unable to get in from Withern.

Memories are Made of This

THE earliest recollections come from <u>Mrs. Kerr</u> who was a pupil in 1904. She remembers it as the British and Undenominational School, the latter part causing many a bad start filling in examination papers. The infants were in a small gallery where they were well grounded in the 3 Rs. Then to Standard I in another classroom where more subjects were taught by a very thorough and strict teacher. If any pupil excelled they were moved to the next Standard, continuing to the highest, Standard VI. The school was noted for teaching a range of subjects, including Algebra, and Biology in the teacher's private room, standing so close together as there was no room for chairs. Sometimes Standards shared a room with a glass partition between from floor to ceiling.

Much enjoyed were Religion and Singing, the latter usually led by a talented pupil with a good voice. "Our headmaster, Mr. Trewick, stood by the huge coke stove to conduct duets and madrigals". Some children's parents paid a small fee, but "we were non-fee paying and were considered a low kind". She had three brothers and a sister attending the school from 5 to 14. There were three playgrounds - infants in front and separate ones at the back for boys and girls. On special days the Union Jack was raised and traditional songs were sung. Drill was taught in the playgrounds. Miss Faulds was in charge of the infants, and Miss Banks from the Technical School in James Street taught cookery.

<u>Mrs. Olive Phillipson (nee Kirk)</u> was born in 1904 and was attending Yarburgh School but the schoolteacher left in 1916 and the school closed for two years. She had to cycle to Kidgate School for those two years (1917-18), returning to

Headmaster:—JOS. TREWICK, A.C.P.

Scholar's Report for Quarter ending April 30 1918

Name of Scholar......Olive Kirk......Standard....Class. I..

Number of Scholars in class....26......Scholar's number in order of merit..........................

Subject.	Possible marks each month.				Remarks.
Reading	12 100	93			
Composition or Dictation	12 100	84			
Handwriting	12 100	82			
Written ⎫ Arithmetic. Mental ⎭	18 100	93			
	12 100	90			
Geography	12 100	78			
English Grammar	12 100	70			
Recitation	12 100	a			
Drawing (boys)	12 100	57			
Needlework (girls)	12 100	92			
Hygiene Physiology	12 100	68			
Algebra	12 100	96			
Euclid (Ex. VII)	12 100	70			
Attendance Gen. Knowledge	12 100	70			
Scripture	100	78			
Total	1600	1123 + 70 History			

Possible marks for Quarter......1600....   Actual marks for Quarter......1123 + 70

Number of times school has been open......148.......

Number of lessons missed on account of absence......102......

Number of times present......114.......   Number of times absent......34.......

Conduct......Excellent......

Signed   J. Trewick P

Headmaster.

Yarburgh for her last term on reaching the age of 14. On one occasion at Kidgate the infants teacher was ill and she was asked to look after the class for the day.

Three of her grandchildren went to Kidgate in the 1960s and 1970s, going on to the Grammar School. Marilyn went to university to study Pure Maths, worked as a tax accountant, married and now lives in Canada; Elizabeth went to Sunderland College and to teach at Ipswich; Andrew went to Sheffield University, read English Literature, became an editor with Macgraw Hill in Maidenhead and wrote "Louth Grammar School - A history" in 1989.

Alec Davey was 14 when he went from Legbourne School to Kidgate for one year in 1917, cycling each day and calling at Jim Humberstone's shop in the village to get 40 aniseed balls for a penny. As well as headmaster Mr. Trewick, he remembers teachers Miss Smith and Miss Faulds, and that the classes were mixed boys and girls. He went to the Technical School in James Street for woodwork, and learnt gardening on the allotments at the end of Wellington Street.

Fred (Bud) Wain went to Kidgate in the late 1920s when it was Senior Mixed. He regularly played truant on Fridays because he loved animals and enjoyed helping to drove the cattle and sheep from the railway station to the market, and had many thrashings as a result. He became a driver with East Lincs Transport, then Wrights buses and the Lincolnshire Road Car. Two of his children, Anne and David, attended Kidgate in the 1940s and 1950s.

Ernest Gibson also attended the Senior Mixed, and remembers moving books on a trolley to the newly built Monks' Dyke School. When he left he worked for Esso at Louth Station for fifty years. His daughter Erica also went to Kidgate (1950-56), won a scholarship and is now a headmistress herself.

When Mrs. Hastead attended Kidgate from the age of five in the 1930s, Percy Latter was the head and he lived in a bay-windowed house next to the school. There was a large school bell hanging high up on the front of the school. Heating was by a big coke stove with a guard round to prevent the children

LINDSEY COUNTY COUNCIL

EDUCATION COMMITTEE

Examination for Junior Scholarships and Exhibitions

MARCH 12th, 1924

ARITHMETIC

Time — 1¾ hours

*Do not attempt more than **eight** questions*

1. Find the total of the following:

tons	cwts.	qrs.	lbs.
62	7	3	2
7	18	1	19
32	13	2	12
4	4	0	21
25	17	3	27

2. Find the least number which when divided by 16, 42, 63, or 72 will leave a remainder of 1.

3. A boy bought a penknife for 2s. 6d. and afterwards exchanged it for 9d. and 210 marbles. How much did he lose supposing the marbles were worth 1d. per dozen?

4. Find the cost of 7 chests of tea each containing 2 qrs. 10 lbs. at £6 2s. 6d. per cwt.

5. How many telegraph poles will be required to support a length of wire 14 miles 3 furlongs 5 chains if the poles are 99 feet apart?

6. A clock loses 5 seconds every 32 minutes. At 10 p.m. on Saturday it is a quarter of an hour fast. When will it be at exactly the right time?

7. If it costs £4 6s. 8d. to feed 13 horses for a week, how much will it cost to feed 3 horses for a year at the same rate?

[Turn over

from getting burnt. "I have seen it red hot on a very cold day", she recalled, "and it was quite scary". For morning assembly the partition was moved back to make a large room. The smaller room had steps across and rising to the windows and the children sat on the steps for lessons. "Once there was a thunderstorm and very dark, and we were all frightened; we were kept in school until the storm had passed".

"We were given the choice of a school uniform, and I remember feeling very proud as I donned the brown gymslip and cream blouse, and a Dutch-shaped hat with the badge of a lion and the letters BS embroidered on it". Despite its new name it was still known as the British School. "I remember taking a penny to school each week to help pay for an extension, a new maternity ward, to Louth Hospital. We had a card with brick shapes and these were marked for every penny collected. Little did I think that six years later I would be working in the hospital".

"My three grandchildren have attended this grand school, one gaining a scholarship. I also took one of my grandchildren on her first day. The teacher standing in the doorway took her hand and said "Do you know, I used to teach your grandma". I wondered just how dear Miss Bontoft must have felt, having taught three generations of one family".

One of the town's and Kidgate's most distinguished scholars was <u>Charles Plumpton</u>. His parents kept a shop in Upgate, and his grandfather had the poultry shop on the corner of Mercer Row and the Market Place. He moved from the Westgate School to Kidgate and remembered with affection Mr. Latter "who tried to be a mathemetician", but hated his one term at Monks' Dyke. A scholarship in 1931, his was the first name on the Honours Board, took him to the Grammar School where he was awarded a County Major Scholarship, a State Scholarship, the Marmaduke Levit Scholarship (best performance in the Cambridge Higher Schools Examination) and an Open Scholarship in Mathematics to St. John's, Cambridge.

There he achieved First Class Honours in Mathematics, the Tyson Medal for Astronomy and a Blue for Association

Football. He served as a radar officer in the RNVR and one of his ships was torpedoed in the North Sea. After a short period in industry and Battersea Polytechnic, he was appointed to the academic staff of Queen Mary College, University of London, serving for 30 years, gaining his PhD in magnethydrodynamics, writing forty books and finishing as Reader in Engineering Mathematics. From 1950 he was deeply involved in schools examination boards as assistant and then Chief Examiner, and established the national core curriculum in "A" level mathematics. He revisited Kidgate School only shortly before he died in 1992.

<u>Harold Jackson</u> attended five village schools - Baumber, Tathwell, Kelstern, Thorganby and North Ormsby (now Utterby) - before attending Kidgate in 1932, aged nine. His sister took him to see the headmaster, Mr. Latter, who asked him one question, "How many beans make five?" "I looked at him astonished," he recalls, "to think he should ask me such a simple question and was speechless. So he put me in Miss Kent's class - the "less bright" children. After a week they thought I would be better placed in Miss Hibbitt's class - the "upper" class. At that time Miss Bontoft taught the infants and Mrs. Broddle the second year."

"My final full year in 1932-33 was in Mrs. Mason's class, all boys. Miss Giddings had the top class for girls. Mrs. Mason lived at Withern; her husband was a farmer and often brought her to school and collected her on his motorcycle. She had a knotted cane, and used it regularly. Every Friday we had an arithmetic test and the top boy was given a medal to wear for a week; it was an embarrassment but if you didn't obey her instructions the knotted cane would remind you."

Strawson Bros. had a jam factory on Cinder Lane in the 1930s. When the children left at 12 o'clock to walk home for lunch, they had to be careful not to get in the way of the mass of girls and women also leaving the factory for their mid-day break - walking, running or cycling.

Harold gained his scholarship, leaving the Grammar School in 1938 to work in Curry's cycle and radio shop in Eastgate. In 1941 he volunteered for the RAF and was drafted to clerical duties because of sight in only one eye. He was posted overseas and Mentioned in Despatches in 1944 for work in organisation and administration of RAF Stations in Southern India. Returning to England in 1945, he married Dorothy Jaines and rejoined Curry's to become a branch manager in Malton, York and Grimsby. He and Dorothy opened a grocery and general store in Church Street in 1950; sadly she died of cancer in 1969 and two years later he sold the business and rejoined Curry's as a stockchecker for England, Scotland and Wales. Then in 1975 he joined T.M. Lusby & Son, agricultural merchants at Saltfleetby until retirement ten years later. He has for a number of years given pleasure to many with his cine and slide shows raising funds for local charities. I am grateful to him for his enthusiastic assistance in compiling and promoting this book.

Pauline Thornton (nee Espin), who was at Kidgate from 1934 to 1940, says her only memories of Mrs. Broddle's class were playing in the percussion band seated on huge mats on the floor, and a visit to the cinema to see a film about how chocolate was made (she won a book prize in a writing and drawing competition about the film). When in Miss Kent's class she remembers sewing lessons and another trip to the Playhouse to see "Snow White and the Seven Dwarfs", Miss Kent having told them about the scary parts beforehand so that they would not be afraid.

"I did little errands for Mrs. Hibbitt", she recalls, "calling at Dorothy's hairdressers on my way home to make an appointment to have her hair iron-waved, for which she would sometimes give me a penny. When the fair was in the Cornmarket and Market Place, she warned us about the dirty and unsavoury people associated with it, and not to go unless with a grown-up. For being late back to school one afternoon after visiting the fair, six girls, including me, were caned by her. Each teacher had a cane, except the earlier classes where they used a ruler. Mrs. Hibbitt's cane had knots in it. We hid the cane if possible; one day it had been dropped behind the large bookcase against the wall and it could not be found when my brother Peter came to borrow it for Mrs. Mason because hers too had "disappeared". On a more pleasant note, I remember being in a play about a group of children who went on a picnic. The highlight was eating the fruit cake Mrs. Hibbitt made for the performance (only pretend eating in rehearsals of course).

"During the very cold winter of 1939-40 the school boiler broke down and the school was closed. The top group preparing for the scholarship examination were taken by Mrs. Mason in Mr. Latter's room upstairs. If he came into our classroom during a singing lesson, she would ask us to sing "Dark brown is the river" because it was his favourite song. During that year I sang in the school choir and we appeared on the stage at the Town Hall.

"In the summer we went to the Maiden Row swimming baths where Mr. Bateson taught us to swim, with a canvas belt round my waist and a long rope held by him. We had to stop using the paddling pool because the soldiers in the town used it for baths, and I remember seeing it filled with steaming soapy water.

"Before the air raid shelters were built, the procedure during a practice or an alert was to file into the cloakroom corridors and sit under the clothes pegs, to avoid any flying glass, although all the windows were cross-crossed with gummed paper. The women were knitting for the troops, and many of us appeared at school with knitted balaclava helmets. I can still visualise the school caretaker, Mr. Good, going down or coming up from the stokehole. The school milk was delivered in churns by Mr. Cribb of Raithby and ladled into enamel mugs on large metal trays by Mr. Good, and all the teachers wore long-sleeved wrap-around dark aprons which tied at the back.

"Some of the games we played in the playground were: The farmer's in his den, I wrote a letter to my love, The wind, the wind blows high, and Statues. Both boys and girls (including me) would drop over the playground wall into Kidgate until it was stopped by Mr. Latter (it was a big drop). We also slid down the handrails on the steep steps down into Springside, and did acrobatics, but this too was stopped after someone fell off and cut their head. We would throw pebbles into the spring and paddle in the shallowest parts of

Springside. We loved to slip down Strawson's Passage from Springside to Queen Street, past the huge vinegar barrels. and sniff the onions pickling and the jam-making smells. Going to and from school was all passages: through the Pack Horse yard, along the passage from Eastgate at the rear of the Liberal Club, into Burnt Hill Lane, through Harness's yard and another passage to Springside and up the steps to Kidgate.

"A popular serial showing at the Saturday matinee (3d at the Palace, 4d at the Playhouse) was Flash Gordon; we would wear our coats inside out and over our shoulders like a cape and be either Flash Gordon or Dale with our toy guns. A painful memory however is of going to the old clinic on Queen Street for dental examination; everyone dreaded it. Later I learned to say "My grandma says I've not to have anything done", but that only saved the day for a time.

"The top ten in Mrs. Mason's class were Sheila Martin (later Greenfield), Donald Winter, Eric Tucker, Rita Addison (later Clapson), Betty Archer, Richard Willerton, Alan Fieldsend, Sylvia Wilson, Michael Dannatt and myself. Donald Winter wore a navy blue suit (short trousers), white shirt and red tie, and his sister wore a navy pleated skirt, white blouse and tie and navy cardigan; was that Kidgate's unofficial school uniform? When we saw the Grammar School girls walking in line along Northgate from school to catch their trains at the station, we would chant: "Grammar School bulldogs, put them in a pen. They can't beat the Kidgate men".

"I remember very clearly" recalls Joyce Mills (nee Towle), "the first day I went to Kidgate Junior School as a pupil teacher; it was September 1935. The headmaster was the jovial kindly Percy Latter (Mr. Latter to us of course), a tall well-built man in smart light grey suit, greying hair and a well-groomed grey moustache, a figure of authority, earning the love and respect of all in his care.

"I was a few months from my eighteenth birthday and had just left the Girls' Grammar School with my Cambridge School Certificate. This would enable me to register as an Unqualified Teacher as soon as I became eighteen. My mother, herself a teacher, was a member of the Schools Management

Board and she chose Kidgate as being the most progressive in the town for me to go to learn the ropes. At that time there were three infant classes with over forty in each of the three classrooms bordering on Kidgate. There was nothing unusual then in being an unqualified teacher, but a woman could be subject to dismissal if she married without first qualifying. A friend who was appointed to Kidgate in 1940 had a difficult time in keeping her job when she married three months later.

"I was placed to observe and work with Miss Elsie Giddings with the middle infants, six-year olds. Each morning the middle class filed into the top classroom and crowded three to a desk, as there was a piano for morning hymns and prayers. It was an embarrassment at first with a hundred pairs of eyes on me; however, I soon became involved, particularly as I played the piano.

"The teachers all wore coat-style wrap-around overalls. I could not think that teaching was such a dirty job, but I made myself a couple just to be one with them. The staff room and head's room were upstairs with a glass-sided walkway along our classroom at roof level. This was very convenient for the head to keep his eye on what we were doing in the classroom. I often noticed him standing up there with his pipe, looking down on us.

"By today's standards, the daily timetable was very structured, but with our periods of individual work and co-operative pictures we were in the forefront. We were allowed three sheets of cardboard a term for these creations: snowdrops in the spring, cutting narrow green strips of gummed paper for the leaves, then on to tulips, crocuses and daffodils. This was part of the afternoon timetable,, nothing so frivolous in the mornings.

"At about 9.40, after prayers and a Scripture lesson, Miss Giddings and I divided the class and took a group each for word building, working from either end of the long wall blackboard. As I worked nearest the road, I could gaze out over the roofs of the town if I became bored, and watch the Market Hall clock slowly move towards ten o'clock when we all went into the playground for PT. Nothing short of pouring rain or too much

102

ice on the sloping yard was allowed to prevent this lesson. On the few occasions when we could not go out the children stood or jumped between the desks and did arms bend and stretch. We then had our daily dose of blackboard teaching of number counting and tables. After playtime from 11 to 12 written maths was done, and English exercises from individual work cards made by the teacher. A start was also made on hearing each child read daily and marking their reading cards. This work always ceased to allow ten minutes singing or poetry before the lunch break (12 noon to 1.30 pm), when practically everyone went home, including me on my bike.

"The afternoon always began with copy writing and letter formation. There were two blue lines in the exercise book to contain the lower case letters and a red line above and below for capital letters. Great care was taken in this writing, copied letter by letter after the teacher had drawn them on the blackboard. Art and craft would follow, and when we were not supervising we could hear a few more read. After playtime, the last three-quarters of an hour was spent finishing the reading, while the children had a choice of plasticine modelling or chalking on small blackboards, and the day finished with a story, drama or music.

"I owe my great love of teaching to my initiation at Kidgate School, and to Miss Giddings, a radiant shining example and the best teacher I ever knew. I wrote in a notebook at the time: "The great help she is giving me may be altogether unknown to her, and this is a proof of how careful we each should be in what we do and say as we never know who may be watching and taking pattern from us." Following her example of kindly but firm discipline I was able to develop her method for myself and became very happy in my teaching.

"In spring 1936 Miss Giddings was taken ill and I was trusted by Mr. Latter to take full charge of her class. I was paid the maximum supply rate of £2 10s a week. There were 48 in the class and I enjoyed the responsibility, carrying on the well established class procedure. I shall always remember my first class at Kidgate; many of them remained in Louth and I still see them, and I can work out their ages as they are twelve years younger than me. Among them were Sylvia Wilson, Beryl Barton, Sheila Martin, Brian Harrison, Alec Cross, Pam Jaines, Pat Perriam, Pauline Espin and Janet Willerton.

"In the summer term Miss Giddings recovered sufficiently to return, although she was terminally ill with cancer and sadly did not live very long. I applied for a vacancy at North Thoresby School to teach infants. Mr. Coles, the headmaster, was impressed with my interview performance and modern methods learned at the Kidgate (Show) School. I got the job but he would not let me visit the school until the other teacher had gone in case I copied some of her habits.

"I never taught at Kidgate again, but my daughter Anne spent a very happy year teaching there in 1972-73 under the headship of Clifford Spray".

John Jaines did not find life at Kidgate very attractive - school lessons did not appeal. He had a lucky escape in September 1941 when his home received a direct hit from a German bomb; seven in the house were killed, including his mother, grandmother and his sister Mary, but John and Margaret were rescued from the rubble. John's younger son Andrew shared his father's feelings about school lessons, but elder son Nicholas worked diligently in the classroom and eventually qualified as a Certified Accountant. John's family haulage business prospered, and father and sons still have a soft spot for Kidgate School.

Roger Marriott, who lived on Kenwick Road, was at Kidgate from 1951 to 1957. When he was about ten, he started breeding white mice and sold them to the local pet shop for a useful profit. He went on to the Grammar School and to Cambridge where he gained a First Class Honours in Economics. He rose through ICI, Unilever and Amcon Group Inc. of New York to become Managing Director of Allegiance Capital, an investment partnership in Stamford, Connecticut.

Mrs Hibbitt's class

MAY 1949

1950

106

1951

107

1952

1953

1954

109

Mr Jackson's class

1955

Back (L-R): *Jennifer Vinter, Catherine Holroyd, Doreen Otley, Fiona Morton, Elizabeth Morton, Mary Hubbard.*

Front: *Michael Pask, Stuart Freshney, Philip Reed, Angus Hatrick, Pauline Robson, Sylvia Cook, Dorothy Willoughby.*

Snow White and the Seven Dwarfs, 1958

as front row above

1965

Back (L-R): *Tim Archer, Robert Dannatt, David Taylor, —, Steven Wrisdale, Paul Stevenson, Stephen Appleby, Linda Kingswood, —, Jane Espin, Janice Brown, John Cowlishaw, —, Keith Norton.* Middle: *Catherine Stroud, Deborah Clark, Paul Webber, —, Julie Barnes, David Fanthorpe, Teresa Doe, Jeremy Holmes, Janet Chapman, Alyn Blythe, David Sharp, Ian Spence, —.* Front: *Susan Breakspeare, —, Janet Bevan, Patricia Guise, Diane Anderson, Miss Rowson, Harry Kerman, —, Mark Gorbutt, —, Kevin Macpherson.*

Back: *Terence Barton, Leslie Bruton, Christopher Goodwin, Michelle Gladwin, Deborah Bonner, Julie Craig, Tony Pettinger, Philip Addison, David Storr, Andrew Johnson, Andrew Tilston, Howard Bramall, Ian Barnes.* Middle: *Deborah Bywater, —, —, —, Alison Lowe, Welch, Miss Hewson, Julie Hall, Pauline Robinson, Sally-Ann Turner, Maria Dixon, Martyn Wyles, Carol Nurse.* Front: *Mandy Oldham, Louise Dunn, —, Rosemary Goy, Lesley Gee, Nicholas Jaines, Martyn Taylor, —, Trudi Skipworth, Linda Nutt.*

1966

Back (L-R): *Diane Anderson, Nicola Barton, Jane Chapell, Caroline Stevenson, Tony Dales, Harry Kerman, Paul Street, Paul Johnson, Trevor Ksrtupelis, Stephen Grundy, —, Tim Archer, Karen Hopley.* 3rd row: *—, Stephen Appleby, John Thompson, David Fanthorpe, David Taylor, Jeremy Holmes, David Sharp, John Cowlishaw, —, Robert Gibbons, Linda Kingswood, Janice Brown.* 2nd row: *Deborah Preston, Patricia Guise, Jane Bevan, Susan Jeffries, Mr Burgess, Martine Gladwin, Maureen Borman, Sorrel Horsestead, Sandra Walmesley.* Front: *Susan Oxley, Janet Taylor, Catherine Stroud, Julie Barnes, Jill Taylor, Lynn Blyth, Sandra Bywater, Lynn Johnson, Margaret Evison.*

1967

Back (L-R): *—, —, Wendy Garbutt —, Keith Norton, Ian Spence, —, Barry Waumsley, —, Simon Loft, —, Rosemary Oxley, —,* Middle: *Espin, —, Christopher Langley, —, Roger Ford, Colin Pearson, Espin, Graham Crowson, Michael Hodkins, —, —,* Front: *centre Mr Oxby, others not known.*

113

CHRISTMAS PARTY 1965

Back (L-R): *Anne Spence, Philip Walmsley, Jane Beeton, —, Anne Chandler, John Appleby,.* Front: *James Loft, Marcus Brown, Carol Nurse, Joyce Evison, Trudi Skipworth.*

First day at school for Christopher and Caroline Morris. 7 September, 1976.

19 June 1975

Christopher Morris, Ian Connell, James Butler.

SPORTS DAY

1976

1st year Infants with Mr Spray (Head) and Mrs Wilson.

1977

1st year Juniors with Miss Finch (student teacher) and Mr Spray.

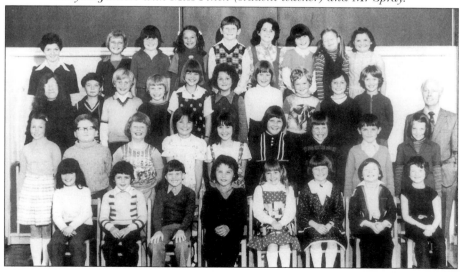

Celebrating 150 Years

THE SCHOOL began its 150th year in September 1990 with the commemorative planting of three apple trees. The apple as the school badge is a reminder that back in 1840 the school had been built in an orchard. The trees were planted by Sarah Jaines, James Whitcombe, Adam Boston, Andrew Brook and Gemma Sharpe, accompanied by the Mayor, Cllr. Joyce Munslow, and the Rector of Louth, Canon David Owen.

The main celebration was in March 1991, that being the month in 1841 when the school first opened. Commemorative items had been produced, including a tea towel,, notelets and a birthday sweatshirt, and the school produced a special edition newspaper - Kidgate News - with contributions from the children. The report STEPPING BACK IN TIME, written by Laura Tunnicliff, Jacqueline Greig, Darren Trafford and Mark Baddon, tells the story.

"We had a great time on March 1! On that day we celebrated Kidgate's 150th birthday.

"The clock was turned back 150 years to the year 1841. Anyone near Kidgate probably got a surprise when they saw little boys wearing knee breeches, waistcoats, jackets, caps, long socks and boots, and little girls in long skirts or dresses with pinafores on top, all running into lines when the school bell was rung. The teachers waited in the playground also dressed in costume.

117

"It was then single file into our classrooms which were re-arranged with desks in rows all facing the blackboard ready to start the day's work. Our lessons were different too, as we saw what schooldays were like for Victorian children. There was drill in the yard, chanting our times tables out loud, learning poetry by heart, reading round the class and religious instruction.

"Some children had the chance to learn copperplate handwriting, and others tried their hand at making corn dollies, doing tapestry work or spinning. Parents were invited to have a peep at the past too.

"When lunch time came we weren't tucking into our usual sandwiches, crisps, chocolate biscuits and yoghurts. A Victorian style lunch was on the menu with soup and a bread roll, baked potato with grated cheese or butter, an apple and a glass of sparkling water.

"The day finished with a special assembly and the cutting of the birthday cake."

Emma Hamilton and Polly Yendell blow out the candles on the birthday cake. (Photo Derrick Furlong)

*Patrick Erkett, Jason Caborn and Daniel Cargill
turn the clock back in the playground on
celebration day. (Photo Derrick Furlong)*

119

School Caretaker Robert Garbutt chats with Scott Kenyeres during the celebrations. (Photo Derrick Furlong)

120

Christopher Brewer, Sarah Mountain, Jemma Bates and Giavanni Frances learn about tapestry from Mrs Linda Jaines.

CELEBRATION DAY

Acting Head Judith Drakes observes the skills of lacemaking in the hands of Mrs Joan Hewson. (Photos Derrick Furlong)

Teaching and other staff, January 1991

Mr. T.H. Thompson   - Headteacher
Mrs. J.A. Drakes   - Deputy Headteacher
Mrs. J. Perkins
Mr. M. Ash
Miss H. Densley
Mrs. A. Chantry
Mrs. R. Cooper
Mrs. P. Powell
Mrs. J. Brown
Mrs. J. Ibberson
Miss J. Ransom
Miss S. Freeston
Mrs. L. Bailey
Mrs. L. Bunce
Mrs. A. Etty

Mrs. J. Brown   - Secretary
Mrs. C. Chambers   - Ancillary Assistant
Mr. R. Garbutt   - Caretaker
Mrs. J. Smith   - Midday Controller

Midday Supervisory Assistants:
Mrs. C. Benson
Mrs. P. Blythe
Mrs. M. Jarvis
Mrs. P. Metcalfe
Mrs. A. Oatway
Mrs. R. Street
Mrs. C. Ward
Mrs. L. Worrell (also Cleaner)

HEADMASTERS

James Seller Forster	1841 -	1851
William Kimm	1851 -	1859
David McMichael	1859 -	1869
Edward Rogers	1869 -	1875
James Hargreaves	1875 -	c.1887
George James Rawson	c.1887 -	1890
John Edward Cheese	1891 -	1894
Joseph Trewick	1894 -	1925
William Forster	1926 -	1929
Percy R. Latter	1930 -	1947
Frank Lamming	1947 -	1955
Clifford Spray	1955 -	1978
T.H. Thompson	1978 -	1991
Stuart M. Sizer	1991 -	

LOUTH BRITISH SCHOOL.

THIS IS TO CERTIFY

THAT

Edward Lindell

WAS EXAMINED BY

HER MAJESTY'S INSPECTOR

and passed successfully

in the 4th Standard on *June 12 1879*

Signed

HONI SOIT QUI MAL Y PENSE